# WHEN TYRANNY TREMBLED

## EDITH HAMILTON

*Best wishes to James Mamanos*

*Edith Hamilton*

DORRANCE & COMPANY
Philadelphia

Copyright © 1974 by Edith Hamilton
*All Rights Reserved*
ISBN 0-8059-2063-3
Library of Congress Catalog Card Number: 74-83922
Printed in the United States of America

To
Second Lieutenant Henry Lunt, USN

# CONTENTS

Page

Foreword ............................................. ix

## PART ONE

**Chapter**

| | | |
|---|---|---|
| 1 | Sons of Liberty | 3 |
| 2 | Henry Lunt and John Paul Jones | 9 |
| 3 | The Tax Performance | 15 |
| 4 | Ezra Lunt | 27 |
| 5 | Cry of Defiance | 33 |
| 6 | Henry Lunt Marries | 39 |
| 7 | The Tavern Meeting | 47 |
| 8 | *Glasgow* Encounter | 54 |
| 9 | After the *Glasgow* | 60 |
| 10 | Visit to Salisbury Point | 65 |
| 11 | Voyage of the *Providence* | 70 |
| 12 | The Privateer *Dalton* | 75 |
| 13 | Old Mill Prison | 81 |

## PART TWO

| | | |
|---|---|---|
| 14 | The *Ranger* | 89 |
| 15 | After the *Ranger* | 98 |
| 16 | The Cruise | 108 |
| 17 | The Battle | 118 |
| 18 | At the Texel | 125 |
| 19 | Flagship *Alliance* | 134 |
| 20 | Back to L'Orient | 144 |
| 21 | Personnel Problems | 152 |

| 22 | The Court-Martial | 161 |
|---|---|---|
| 23 | Home on the *Ariel* | 170 |
| 24 | Honors from Congress | 177 |
| 25 | The *America* | 187 |
| 26 | The Tolls of War | 199 |

## APPENDICES

| A | Nathaniel Tracy | 211 |
|---|---|---|
| B | Letters Documenting Jones's Trip to Newburyport | 212 |
| C | The Privateer *Dalton* | 214 |
| D | The Treaty of Alliance with France, 1778 | 218 |
| E | The American Squadron | 219 |
| F | On the Death of John Paul Jones Eighty-five Years After | 220 |
| G | Old South Church | 221 |
| H | Tristram Dalton | 222 |
| I | Dr. Ezra Green | 223 |
| Bibliography | | 224 |

## Foreword

The account of events related in the following pages is all true and has been carefully researched.

Where direct quotes are used, poetic license has been taken in order to color a picture of colonial times and idioms.

The people named here really lived and did perform as here told. There are letters and documents in archives to substantiate this, and if there are any who would care to follow the same trail, the markers are waiting in institutes and libraries the length of the New England coastline and in Washington, D.C.

The service of Second Lieutenant Henry Lunt with Commodore John Paul Jones is public record. The author believes, however, that this is the first time events have been drawn up in such fine and intimate detail.

It is to be hoped that this book will find its place in time and will bring both information and enjoyment to those now pausing for celebration and remembrance of the American Revolution two hundred years later in the 1970s.

Edith Hamilton

*Part One*

# 1

## SONS OF LIBERTY

On the night that was to change his life, young Henry Lunt walked whistling into the chill of an early December evening. The snow was sifting down softly and effortlessly, and it seemed to brighten the darkness that fell early in winter. Lunt welcomed the wet snow upon his face and lips, still heated from the glow of the open fire and hot rum cup he had tasted before venturing forth. His waistcoat and breeches felt snug from hearty indulgence in his mother's good meal of mush and molasses and apple tart. But, never mind, he would use it all up in the walk of several miles from the Newbury Lower Green to Newburyport Towne at the mouth of the Merrimack River.

Winding before him the width of a farm wagon was the High Road, and as Henry moved past an occasional house, candles flicked from small-paned windows in friendly greetings. Snow thundered off a sloping roof making him jump, but no voice called to join up with him, and no dark silhouette loomed on the road ahead. It seemed evident that he was the last to head into town for the meeting at the tavern.

Having no wish to be late, Lunt began to move with increasing swiftness until he was running, easily and lightly, as one brought up with the deer paths and furrowed fields of the colonial times in which he lived. The highway became straighter, and he could hear the pounding surf at Plum Island a mile away on his right. Houses grew closer together on either side, and, as he sped by them, the candle lights were winking out. Already the children were being bedded for an early routing at the first light.

As the Newbury man turned into Fish Street, he could make

out the swinging lanterns outside the Wolfe Tavern.* Further on, he could hear the creak of metal hinges, and soon he could see the huge, wooden, oval sign with its cut of a man in a three-cornered hat; adjacent printing assured the traveler that his host was James Wolfe, Esq., who offered warming food, drink, and lodging.

Avoiding the wide door of the front entrance, Henry Lunt moved instead to the dark side door leading to the hospitable tap room. He stamped his booted feet to rid them of snow. Nevertheless, snow followed and swirled all about him as he entered the vestibule, also dark and very damp. He unwound from his head, and then from his neck, a long, woolen scarf before doffing his three-cornered hat and seaman's greatcoat. Shaking them of snow, he hung them together on a ready wooden peg in line with many others on either side of the narrow outer room. Then, to avoid a chill, he moved swiftly into the cheery, lamp-lit hospitality room.

The room was long, seeming narrow although it was not, and it had a smell most curiously intermingling wet, musky garments, laced cider, and tallow. Christmas greens that had lost their aroma festooned the walls, even over the narrow mantel of the huge fireplace where a blaze of incredible dimensions was being sucked up a wide chasm of chimney. The fire, plus human breath and sweat, provided the only warmth the room afforded.

Lunt saw that he was probably the last to come of those expected. Already, there were so many men crowded into the room some were standing against the walls. Going first to the fire to warm his face and hands, the Newbury man gave greeting where it was met by those he knew. He then moved to a prominently placed table where he saw that a seat had been saved for him on one of the benches—by virtue, he thought proudly, of being a brother to Ezra. That brother, taller by half a head, had risen to greet Henry. They solemnly shook hands. Henry then seated himself beside his second eldest brother, Captain Daniel Lunt, a handsome, blonde giant.

There were six men by the name of Lunt at the same table; the

---

* See Bibliography, item 12.

other three being brothers—Richard, Paul, and Cutting, with ages in that order—who were cousins of Henry and his brothers. All were members of the Sons of Liberty, an organization of young men brought into being—so they declared—"by the most grievous persecutions of King George III of England and his evil doers on American earth."

It was in the closing days of the year 1773, and the awesome truth was becoming prevalent: an American revolution with all of its bloody connotations was surely in the offing. Ezra Lunt, one of the publishers of *The Essex Journal and Merrimack Packet*, a local newspaper, had been selected for a role of leadership. His topic tonight was taxation without representation, with special emphasis upon the tax on tea.

Ezra made several attempts to open the meeting, but it seemed that a spirit of jubilation among some of the younger men had preceded him. They were boisterous and celebrating to a point of danger, Ezra thought, fearful that the enemy without would hear. But the tavern walls were thick and the storm was noisy. Besides, it was the Christmas season. A half smile creased his stern lips as he listened to the talk bantering about him.

The tea party of Boston was on everyone's lips, and there was great admiration for the men and boys who had pulled it off. "Disguised as Indians, they were, and they dumped a whole cargo of tea into Boston Harbor." Cutting Lunt, brandishing his small pewter cup, stood on a bench. "Over half the men and boys in all of Boston Town were there to have a hand."

Ezra knew better than this, having ridden half the day to bring the news from Charlestown. Well, let their spirits run high. They would wane soon enough in the dread struggle of the days ahead. Nevertheless, it was time to get down to business. He caught Cutting's eye and brought him back to his seat.

Ezra now had near order, but Joe Stanwood persisted in beating up a fine noise on his drum, which was with him wherever he went. He was a fine drummer, and his friends were toasting him with gusto as they kept calling for "one more roll in the name of free men."

Henry Lunt, while sympathizing with Ezra, beat time with his foot to the riffle of the drum. His spirits were high for a personal reason, for he had, this day, received his master's ticket and would sail as captain of a merchantman as soon as the weather allowed. Henry was now equal in rank to his older brother, Daniel, who, without an envious bone in his body, tonight welcomed the other most joyously as an equal.

Ezra was frowning now. In a momentary lull, he sprang to his feet, shaking a raised fist, and loudly confided to a near kinsman, "I am shaken indeed by those who seem to think survival's planning is naught but sport when we have but fearful times ahead."

The displeasure of their leader and his words of reproach found their mark. The noise diminished and died. Soon, every eye in the room was on Ezra, and he saw that the meeting could begin.

The roll was carefully called, and all dark corners of the great room were filled with light so that every man could make certain of his neighbor. James Bragg drew the short straw, making him a disgusted, shivering watch by the outer door, lest king's men take them by surprise. Even then, who knew which man among them might turn traitor?

Conviviality was at an end as each visage turned speculatively cold and grim.

The sailors of the sea, including the Lunt cousins, felt a chill of uneasiness at this quick change of attitude. In the past, they had attended such meetings infrequently and hardly ever altogether. Only the Christmas holidays had brought about this happenstance. These men were courteous in their attention but impatient that Ezra focused concern more on the problems of merchants and manufacturers, who, any seaman knew, were rich beyond belief and were always the big gainers when the ships came in with cargo from the Indies.

The seamen had more concern for the plight of American sailors stolen from the small, defenseless, merchant ships and pressed into British naval service as well as for the plundering of these vessels. The fervor of their protestations provided a wedge which would later take hostilities to sea in open warfare. Tonight, theirs was a voice scarce heard as the burden of unfair taxation became the issue.

While feeling neglected, the sailors dutifully thumped the table when called upon for unanimity. Only Henry Lunt was disturbed enough to show it, for his unswerving interest was always aboard ship in a dedication to duty bordering upon fanaticism.

Daniel Lunt, who longed only for a peaceful life and long stays at home between voyages, fervently hoped there would be no need for armed opposition at sea. With an eye on Henry and their lively cousin Cutting, who shared Henry's views with good nature, Daniel prodded them to silence on the sea issue.

Therefore, before the meeting ended, even Henry and Cutting had committed some of their time on land to the political activities of the Sons of Liberty. Most members of the organization were employed in some way by the mercantile leaders of Newburyport, and they left it to their providers to work out the finer, legal aspects of their cause. Because of this, both interest and enthusiasm waned when Ezra attempted to equate them with late developments in the colonies of the crown to the south. There were few and faint huzzahs when it was announced that first steps had been taken for a channel of communication from north to south. It was a step, furthermore, to set up a skeleton government within the framework of independence. Nevertheless, they had the news, and Ezra's duty was discharged when he informed them that the first Committee of Safety and Correspondence had been appointed by the House of Burgesses in Virginia. But these northern activists could not perceive the usefulness of such a committee and turned it down as an effort to split the ranks of the Sons of Liberty. When it was later put to the town fathers of Newburyport, they would be quick to see the worth.

For the first time, the Sons of Liberty disappointed Ezra Lunt, and he was later to realize that few of his members had qualities of leadership to equal his own. The common man, even though many had had to earn the right to be free men, had yet to learn all that would be demanded of him in his efforts toward change.

Daniel, recognizing his brother's total chagrin, made haste to soothe him with reminders of the lateness of the hour and waning interest in the cup. This largest member of the Lunt family took the good natured approach to discipline and was one of the most popular of the sea masters at the port. At Daniel's invitation, a toast to Ezra was drunk, and with that the meeting ended. The heat from the roaring fire and the human exhalation, combined with plentiful imbibing of mulled cider, had temporarily exhausted their spirits.

Suddenly, from the area of the hearth came the sound of loud snoring—John Coates had fallen asleep. Those nearest immediately punched and shouted him awake and bore him away. And so, it was a jovial parting.

After taking leave of his married brothers who resided in Newburyport, Henry set out for his father's home in Newbury. Riding post behind the saddle of his cousin Paul Lunt, they trotted the High Road in silence, each withdrawn into his own thoughts—Paul the landsman and Henry, master of the sea.

It was not a happy ride for Henry Lunt. Gone was his exuberance of early eve as he evoked melancholy thoughts of his life at sea being swept away should he be compelled to war on land. He lifted his face to the night and freed his lips from his muffler to taste the chill wine of the falling snow. His mouth felt dry and his stomach sour, which added to his discontent.

As he breathed in the purging elements and his lungs felt lighter, his thoughts grew brighter, and by the time the horse with its double burden arrived at the Lower Green in Newbury, Henry was resolute. He looked to the sky and saw the moon emerging from out the clouds.

He told himself, "Why, how could I fight on land if it comes to that?" He almost shouted it aloud. "How could I, a sailor, fight anywhere but in a navy?" He answered himself. "We have no navy and are not likely to have. England would never stand for it!"

And even as his lips framed the words of his silent protest, his intuition gave a strange and uneasy answer. "A way will be found, Henry Lunt. There will be a navy, and you will fight in it!"

2

# HENRY LUNT AND JOHN PAUL JONES

*HENRY LUNT*

Henry Lunt was born to his shivering mother on a bitter winter day in a great farm kitchen. The midwife held him by his heels and whacked his bottom pink (although he did not need it) while he shrieked in indignation. There was little warmth to be had from the fireplace on that day of February 16, 1753, and the large clapboard house was only about twenty degrees warmer than the freezing outside temperature.

Matthew Lunt, warmed in his heart by the joy of a third son after two daughters, hardly felt the cold. He fondly caressed the cheek of his wife, Jane, lying in exhausted sleep on the harsh straw mattress of their rope bed. Taking the new born babe from the place beside her, he carried him across the room to a like bed where his two sons, Ezra, ten, and Daniel, eight, huddled together under homespun coverlets, frightened by all that had happened before their eyes.

Matthew looked down upon them and showed them their new brother. Revealing his disappointment in them, perhaps more than he intended, he said, "Now, may the two of you pursue your separate ways, for I have here a son who shall till the soil after me."

If, at that moment of tooth-chattering fear and awakening joy, the two boys comprehended what their father was saying, they must have experienced a shared sense of relief.

Small, serious Ezra, who even then cared more for learning and the making of letters, and slow, happy Daniel, flogged at least three times a week for overstaying at the Newburyport wharves, certainly welcomed this new brother as one who would deliver them from the bondage of life on a farm, which each in his own way abhorred.

Matthew Lunt was doomed to another disappointment, and his dream of a son to stay with the farm was not to be. Henry, from the first stubbornly determined to follow the sea, was not to be denied. Matthew found this third son to be twice the handful of his two brothers put together. Henry, named for the sire who first settled in Newbury, was from the first obsessed with ships and how to make them sail. He became Daniel's shadow, and now Matthew had double the chore of keeping them at home.

The sea was in their blood. Henry was only eight when Daniel, at sixteen years of age, left home to apprentice to the master of a merchantman. Soon the older boy was at sea in fast voyages to and from the West Indies. The younger boy fumed and fussed because he could not go along. He felt as old as Daniel in dedication to the sea and clung ever harder to his determination to follow.

Henry was only a year old when the decisive French and Indian War began, and it was in an atmosphere of suspense and dread that he grew up. People, men especially, were constantly coming and going in his life, and some never did return again. It might be said that his was a generation never removed from war's demands. Even the America he knew, although still loyal to mother England and her desires, moved ever closer to rebellion and revolution.

In their very young years, the Lunt children were never allowed to move unescorted far from their own fields, lest Indians pounce upon them to carry them away into slavery far off in Canada. As was inevitable, the boys formed opinions and prejudices, with special resentment of all persons French—an attitude which Henry, alone, would later overcome. It was necessary for all, even the girls, to learn to shoot with unerring accuracy, and this they did with musket and blunderbuss. Most of the time the latter threw them on their backs from the force of recoil and greatly diminished a second chance of survival.

There was a tiny schoolhouse at the Lower Green in Newbury, not far from the Lunt homestead. There, the children of Matthew and Jane spent a couple of hours each day learning to read, write, and cipher. This education, although scanty, was regarded as a luxury by most and certainly enough by their father.

Matthew Lunt labored diligently to turn Henry from the sea, and without compunction he enlisted the aid of family, friends, and clergy. He used every known blandishment, even those of total disinheritance.

It was of no use. Henry remained undefeatable. When he saw that he was beset on all sides, he appeared to yield to his father, and he did the farm chores and worked the fields just so long as someone kept an eye on him. But he would run away as often as he could, and always he would turn up on the wharves at Newburyport. Ezra had been alerted to watch for his brother, and he enlisted the aid of all who knew him to keep him posted. Due to the diligence of these friends, Ezra was able to collar Henry and cart him home. While his kinsfolk were only serving to frustrate him, they probably saved the young boy from making a rash choice of masters and indenture to some unscrupulous rascal.

It finally became evident that to oppose a lad so infatuated with the sea was foolhardy. Matthew Lunt, while still protesting his bitter disappointment, conceded that elders seem to have little control over youth's feverish desires. However, once he had yielded, he went all of the way.

Henry, much to his surprise and delight, began to receive cooperation. During the remainder of the 1760s, he was permitted to dedicate a large portion of his time to the study of sailing ships, from the hewing of the ribs in the forest to the raising of the hulls on the ways. By the time the year 1770 had rolled around, Henry had passed his sixteenth birthday. He was then apprenticed to a merchant master who, in the manner of custom, became his only teacher. Soon, Henry, always an eager learner, was well beyond the fundamentals. Almost at once, he could handle the sheets, shoot up a rope ladder, and walk the yards with as much ease as he could walk the streets of town. He took readily to the study of stars, wind, and ocean currents until he was a master of navigation. His teacher was well satisfied and made such glowing reports to Matthew Lunt that the father began to favor his decision to allow Henry to go to sea.

Matthew, likewise, was relieved that he had not indulged in the temptation to send Henry to sea with Daniel, for there was too much affection between the brothers to permit a proper discipline. It was then believed that all boys must have a flogging on occasion or at least be denied a Sunday pudding. Daniel could never have restricted his brother in such a manner, for he was well known for producing the laziest cabin boys on the line.

An aura of destiny seemed to hover over Henry. He shed not a tear that one could see when he moved from the shelter of parental love and care to the cold comfort of a damp pallet on the floor of his master's cabin and to the tasteless diet of salt sea rations. All of this was a prelude, and when the hour of his country's need came, Henry Lunt was ready. What could not be foreseen was that he would meet up with John Paul Jones and gladly follow in the wake of a seaman no greater than himself, but one who had an unmistakably greater personality that could inspire men to deliver beyond their abilities.

## *JOHN PAUL JONES*

If there is a destiny which shapes men's ends, and there oft times seems to be, that of Henry Lunt was shaped six years before his birth in a country far across the Atlantic Ocean where another boy was born. John Paul Jones, whose early aims and experiences followed a pattern similar to those of Henry Lunt, was born on July 6, 1747, son of a gardener on the estate of the Earl of Selkirk at Abigland on the Firth of Solway. Scotland. He was born John Paul, but for reasons known only to him, he added later the name of Jones.

Henry Lunt was sixteen when he went to sea, but John Paul Jones was only twelve. He apprenticed to an American sea captain on the merchant ship *Friendship*. Scheduled to serve for seven years in order to become a qualified ship's officer, John was fortunate in that his master was a kind, willing, and able teacher. It was probably this early association which instilled in the boy a general liking for Americans.

His first voyage was to Virginia, where his brother, William, had settled and prospered. Encouraged by William, John studied maritime books and books on navigation. With an attention to detail, he learned of the handling of all types of sailing ships.

William had no children, and he invited his younger brother to remain with him to learn about the land. He was well pleased when he discovered that John had a ready mind and a natural aptitude for gentlemanly behavior. The boy, on the other hand, had already been won over to the sea. There was a wildness in his nature that could be identified with a chase before the wind. He loved the tumultuous activity of chomping sheets, groaning masts, and thundering sails. He thrilled to the testing of strength against a ship's wheel on a slanting, tipsy deck.

John Paul Jones knew no greater ecstasy than that which accompanied the stepping from his quarters into the weather. That is, if he was met with the smells and sights of a clean and tidy ship. This was a trait for which he was well remembered by both his officers and people. If some labeled his nagging and fault-finding a pseudo-perfectionism, all aboard his ship soon learned one important lesson: when a vessel was to be hoed down and overhauled, and that was often, officers as well as men had to turn to and help.

In a day when ships were allowed to become fouled with vermin and rot, John Paul Jones was something of a curiosity, and he was frequently scorned as womanish by less fastidious sea captains. He was often accused of dereliction of duty in order to indulge his finicky nature.

Ignoring their criticisms, Jones was won't to cry, "We must have a respecktable navy, or, alas, America!"

Ever restless, John Paul Jones served for a time in the British Royal Navy, but he couldn't tolerate a caste system in which a gardener's son could not rise to the top. He shipped as second mate aboard a slaver. In passage from Jamaica to Kercubright in 1768, both master and mate took sick and died, and Jones was forced to assume command of the vessel. He brought her safely to her destination and was rewarded by being made her master. Afterward he made several voyages to the West Indies.

John Paul Jones forever regretted this period in his career. He was no doubt relieved when it was cut short, but he hardly felt proud of the circumstances under which he severed his connections with the slave trade. An insubordinate officer drew his sword and Jones was forced to defend himself. The other man was killed, calling for an official investigation. Not wishing to become involved, the governor of the island turned his back while the young captain fled—to Virginia at last.

It was around this time that John Paul added the name of Jones. His reason for this never has been determined. It has been hinted that he was the illegitimate son of a Scottish nobleman. Some have said he took the name of an American who befriended him after his brother called him to task for casting a blemish on his family name.

John Paul Jones settled in Virginia in the year 1773. His brother, William, died, and John inherited, becoming for a brief time a member of the southern gentry. He found the entire countryside ablaze with indignation over the treatment of the thirteen colonies by the mother country.

The fiery words of Patrick Henry, shouted from the floor of the Virginia House of Burgesses eight years before, were now on every lip. "Give me liberty or give me death!" cried every patriot with all his heart.

Inspired by the patriotism of these Virginians, Jones was influenced to join them. He began to dream of a role in defense of America at sea, and, with his penchant for the dramatic, he soon saw himself as a leader in the founding of an American navy where a caste system wouldn't frustrate the ambitions of a worthy and dedicated candidate. He saw an American navy to challenge in size and grandeur that of England, the admitted mistress of the seas.

But, before all this could happen, the thirteen British colonies of America would have to wait until they had toiled through all of the vicissitudes and reckless actions that led to revolution.

## 3

## THE TAX PERFORMANCE

Henry Lunt was eleven years old in 1764, the year King George III and his supporters in the English Parliament demanded that the thirteen American colonies pay a share of the debt incurred during the French and Indian Wars. As usual, there were opposing views. The crown maintained that it had acted to protect the colonists from invasion by France. The Americans protested that the war had been a power play between the two great nations, using both Canada and the colonies as a ploy.

Their appeals for a hearing quickly denied, the colonial assemblies were asked for monetary contributions, which they promptly refused to give. Parliament then proceeded to level a tax, its exponents shrewdly maneuvering the Americans into a position of paying up or defying the government—the latter punishable as treason.

In an amazing short time the news was spread throughout the colonies. Their retaliation was also shrewd. Wise leaders of the protest movement cautioned against acts of violence and public displays. Instead, they sent a communication to Parliament declaring the time had come for the states to have their representatives in Parliament, and, until this was accomplished, the colonies could not recognize "taxation without representation."

It was stalemate only momentarily. From that time on, events began to move toward separation and an American revolution.

The years leading up to separation were very prosperous ones for the people of the Merrimack Valley area and Newburyport in particular. This small New England seaport, located thirty-five miles from Boston, moving north over the hills as the crows fly, flourished both grandly and graciously.

Only a century before there had been blank wilderness, until the settlers came up the Parker River from Ipswich to found the Towne of Newbury. The port came later as the need for trade arose, and the larger town at the mouth of the broader Merrimack River mushroomed rapidly.

Newburyport was a narrow town, stretching thinly along the south bank of the Merrimack and looking out on the sea. The river's mouth yawned deceptively wide as it pressed to the Atlantic Ocean, for its navigable channel was narrow, containing well-concealed treachery in rip tides and changing shoals. The channel tides moved swiftly and with great force across a sandy bar. Even those familiar with its habit of shifting shoals were sometimes caught and sent to their doom in their white-sailed ships within sight and sound of home. Still, the sea was the town's very life and was the reason for its fair renown as a mercantile center the world over.

Of prime importance to Newburyport was the trade carried on with the French West Indies. Handsome ships of lofty sails called merchantmen were built in the port, and it maintained supportive industries and, of course, the several shipbuilding yards. There were occupations and work enough for all, and all were expected to work.

The countryside in outlying Newburyport was rich in farm lands for the raising of livestock and garden produce. Verdant forests for fuel, lumbering, and milling stretched hundreds of miles to the north and to the back country moving west.

Industry was gathered at the port where excitement teemed about the Market Square and adjacent wharves. The rank smells of rotten fish and the tar barrel vied with the good smells of spices, molasses, and ships' timbers smoked in sun and salt. Frequently, all of these were overwhelmed by the smell of the east wind, wet with the sea, that assailed the nostrils and drove the breath back down one's throat. Hailed for its cooling relief in summer, a wind "gone easty" was cursed in winter for a chill that could penetrate any garment or any living-structure.

Established as a major seaport in the colonies, Newburyport built sailing ships which were the envy of mariners the world over. Particularly envious were English builders.

In the building of the Newburyport ships, no expense was spared. San Domingo mahogany, a luxury wood soon to become scarce, was used without thought of the morrow for planking and rails. Life-sized figureheads, hand carved from wood from the Rowley joiner's shop, loomed brilliantly painted high on hulls, safe under the bowsprits.

Principal customers for these ornate vessels were merchants of England who usually paid for them, not with money, but with manufactured goods and with produce from the British West India Islands. As time went on, the Newburyport mercantile community began to resent such trade agreements, fanned the more by their rising discontent with the governing by the mother country.

Matthew Lunt came often to the Newburyport Market Square, and all of his children looked forward to accompanying him in the great farm wagon drawn by four horses. The market was a fascinating place, usually crowded with both buyers and sellers, but particularly so when a ship came in with a cargo from the Indies.

Back country buyers from New Hampshire flocked by wagon and river gundalow to the Newburyport market place. There they traded farm produce, meat on the hoof, wool, timber, and distilled spirits for English calico and Spanish cutlery, and West Indian molasses, sugar, and spice.

Beef and pork, costing but little to raise, lumber, salt, and northern water fish were all exchanged at Spanish Martinique or St. Vincent for molasses, sugar, cotton, and indigo. For practical purposes, Newburyport did not use the lavish, beautiful ships for trade, but built, instead, small inexpensive vessels that could sail in and out of her treacherous harbor with less chance of fouling on the bar at the mouth of the Merrimack.

Discontent began to pile on discontent. Soon, the merchants of England began to yield to their greed and to look longingly on this side affair her New England colonies had by then established in trade with other countries, especially France. English politicians began to nag that they should, and could, supply all such goods from nearby Jamaica and Barbados.

Earlier, Parliament had laid duties on the importation of sugar and molasses by Massachusetts, but these never had been systematically collected. It was suddenly decided that these acts of trade should be strictly enforced. The green god had done his work. Permissive paternalism changed overnight to belligerent intolerance.

Men who would fight in the American Revolution were mere boys when the storm clouds began to gather, and their attitudes of resentment, fanned by their elders, were to grow up with them. In the thick of this, by virtue of generations behind them, was the large family of Lunts.

For the sake of the role they would play in the Revolution, it is necessary to recount the sequence of events leading up to this. Local affairs obscured for a time the seriousness of the differences between England and the northern seaport.

Newburyport was incorporated as a town on the twenty-eighth day of January, 1764, which meant peaceful and agreeable separation from Newbury, the old town.

That same year, Lord Granville declared his intention of deriving new revenue from America by increasing the duties on molasses and sugar. British naval commanders were made revenue officers authorized to intercept American vessels and stop trade between the colonies and the French West Indies.

The Americans considered this a blow beneath the belt. The duties being imposed raised objections in all parts of New England, inland as well as on the seacoast. There were threats of other measures to come. Many of the colonists had near relatives and friends back home in England. By exchange of letters came information that a plan was under consideration by Parliament to change the entire structure of the colonial government. This plan was called, "An Act for better regulating His Majesty's Colonies in America."

In common with communities far and wide, the people of Newburyport called a mass meeting to register disapproval, and they instructed their representative to the General Court of Massachusetts to so do.

Their representative, Dudley Atkins, Esq., was, in particular, to use all of his influence in opposing the Stamp Act as one of the major implements burdening and obstructing trade. The Stamp Act, they claimed, was of concern to all, rich and poor alike. Land could not be conveyed, a ship cleared, a suit instituted, an action laid, a marriage entered into, a legacy bequeathed, an orphan's guardianship secured, unless stamped paper, vellum or parchment, was used in recording several writings of the same piece. No writing was valid which did not bear on its face the stamp.

The Stamp Act contained 55 clauses with 200 particular cases in which stamp duties must be paid, varying in value from a half penny to six pounds. Other articles besides paper were subject.

They resented paying the money, but, more than this, the overriding objection to the tax was its encroachment on their time, energies, and social existence. The tax was an unwanted intruder, hampering the business of life itself. It had stirred up the dust in the peaceful lanes of home and riled the tranquil waters of the coastal lanes at sea.

In anger and frustration, the town fathers of Newburyport directed that no citizen should take on the task of distributing the stamped papers, "at the risk of incurring the displeasure of the towne." Hot tempered members of the Sons of Liberty rose to the occasion by hanging the potential tax collector in effigy at the foot of Federal Street east of Market Square. The dummy remained hanging for forty-eight hours, after which, when spirits were cooler, it was dropped into a bonfire kindled below. This time, a mob gathered and roamed the town streets. Persons thought favorable to the Stamp Act were hustled from their homes and forced to witness the burning.

Level-headed townsmen were worried. They retrenched and sought the support of their clergy that the "better nature of man should be served, while, at the same time, his rights protected." This was a large order for God to deliver through his intermediaries, but on that occasion He did it. Against the ranks of those who upheld the Almighty, the rioters ran out of steam—at least for the time being.

The Stamp Act was passed in March and due to take effect in November, but even persons most loyal to the king were so intimidated that neither distributors nor stamps were to be found in the Towne of Newburyport. Before the year ended, the act was formally appealed.

The Newburyport residents celebrated by illuminating the town house and discharging six and one-half barrels of gunpowder from cannon set up on the upper and lower long wharves.

The Stamp Act's repeal served to quiet the people for a while. However, the continuing duties upon goods and ships and the harassment of sailors began again to raise temperatures. What was more, the pocketbooks of merchants were being hard hit.

In September, 1768, in answer to a letter from Boston, Newburyport sent a representative to confer with the "Committee of the Province." The subject under deliberation was, "To Ascertain the best means of securing the peace and safety of the people of Massachusetts." The most important proposition to come out of this Boston meeting was the one suggesting that merchants agree not to import any goods from Britain or her dependents while the existing duties remained. This proposal asked a lot.

Americans very much needed the goods that were to be banned. They included such articles as paper, pasteboard, white and red lead, nails, saltpetre and other items—goods the colonies were not permitted by law to manufacture for themselves. Saltpetre, it might be noted, is one of the main components of gunpowder.

Leaders of Newburyport mostly favored the boycott but feared the rank and file might not accept it. Reluctant to revive the street demonstrations, they decided for the moment to adopt a wait-and-see attitude—to "depend upon every loyal Patriot to use his own judgment." Positive or punitive action on the suggestions of the Boston Committee was set aside.

No decision proved to be its own decision. Grumblings behind the door continued and, as in all like cases, bred an undercurrent of discontent stronger than might have been so. People seemed to favor goods imported from England more than ever. This brought them no rewards from across the water. In fact, penalties for infractions of the rules became tougher. Small reports grew to unsubstantiated rumors of enormous size. It was evident that the Newburyport leaders could no longer duck the issue.

A full year had passed before, on September 4, 1769, at a meeting brought together and aroused by fiery speakers, the people passed a vote denouncing all importers of British goods as enemies to the liberties of the country. Likewise, it was promised to pursue all constitutional measures to compel them to desist.

The shrewdness in the framing of this measure is seen in that it was leveled by Americans at Americans and could be, in no way, misconstrued as treasonous against the crown. As a result, frightened Loyalists, fearing for their own safety, consulted their intelligence sources both in America and in England.

Once more, the desired result was obtained. All duties were subsequently repealed—excepting the one on tea.

The decade of the seventies had come in on a roaring voice of change. Sides had been drawn up, and men knew with clarity where they and other men stood on the issue of independence. A desperation of purpose was moving the thirteen colonies into a greater unity, one with the other. There were contributing factors which silenced those who would oppose.

One of these concerned the method used to collect the set revenues of the crown. British army officers, unaccustomed to such chores, were appointed collection agents. Many abused their authority and tacked on higher interest rates than the law demanded and promptly pocketed the difference. Any person who opposed or appealed this outrage was put in jail and held there until he agreed not to prosecute.

The Sons of Liberty retaliated by turning on those of their neighbors thought to be loyal to the king. They spied on the movements of these men, and woe betide anyone suspected of being an informer. He was roughly seized, even within the walls of his own home, dragged through the streets, and most times tarred and feathered. The activities of the Sons of Liberty, although intended for common good, aroused the disgust of many townsmen who were otherwise dedicated to the cause of freedom.

It was at this point in time that condition came close to getting out of hand. Leaders of north shore communities, in an act of diplomacy, began to make diplomatic approaches to the Sons of Liberty.

Meanwhile the tax on tea remained. The scheming colonists, this time with the cooperation of the Sons of Liberty, seized upon the tax to dangle a series of acts to be used as red herrings across the path of revolution—their real intent. So well did they do their work, so whole hearted was the cooperation they received, so guarded was the secret of their true purpose many latter day historians missed what was really a great trick.

On March 5, 1774, while the Boston Massacre of 1770 was being recalled with memorial services everywhere, the day was ushered in at Newburyport with the tolling of church bells. A morning meeting was held at eleven o'clock in the First Presbyterian Church with an appropriate sermon by its pastor, the Reverend Jonathan Parsons. In the evening, church bells were tolled again.

Something else happened during that emotional March memorial. The ladies of Newburyport held serveral tea parties, simultaneously, where they served various concoctions known as "liberty tea," brewed of sage or ginger or a local herb. These concoctions tasted bad, like anything but tea, and served to increase their discontent all the more.

This constant whining and weeping over the tax on tea, coupled with the masochistic antics of the colonials, made them the laughing stock of the English on both sides of the ocean. Even so, their activities increased and, in spreading rumor about, engaged in tall tales, such as the overturning of tea tables by wild bulls and hair-pulling contests among the ladies.

There were actual events of more telling impact carried on by the men, and tea was burned publicly in the market places of many communities, including that of Newburyport. It is to be remembered that there was a legitimate complaint. Shiploads of tea were forced upon merchants against their wills, and they were forced to pay for it.

Meetings were held in all the towns of the New England mercantile center, ostensibly to discuss the tax on tea. Portions of the minutes of these meetings are a matter of public record. Their other discussions can be learned only with endless picking at the pages of letters and archives. What then comes to light is a series of well-timed movements of cannon, shot, guns, powder, and other ordnance to strategic points.

While some of the members of Parliament were laughing, others were sober of countenance and uneasy. More knowledgeable of their American brethren, and familiar with their maneuvers borrowed from the wily American Indian, they warned their fellows of overconfidence. Their warnings were ignored, and the king took further action.

Selected for punishment, the larger port of Boston was closed to all incoming and outgoing trade. The seat of government in Massachusetts was transferred to Salem. This gave the Patriots cause for worry. Not because of the privation and hardship imposed on the people of Boston—these were nothing new to the hardy sons of the wilderness—but for a different and more important reason. Military stores were concealed at Concord, twenty-five miles westward, but a greater worry was the larger cache at Charlestown within the barricaded area.

It seemed at this point that just about everything justified the viewpoint of the king's advisers: England had the matter well contained. She had succeeded in stifling the American economy by crippling her trade, and she had a large, standing army in America with revenue officers at every port, including Newburyport.

It was in the fateful year of 1774 that Parliament passed an act totally subverting early charter rights, the principal points of the bill aimed directly at the Massachusetts Bay.

Ezra Lunt galloped on horseback to Salem and returned on the same day to Newburyport to bring the news to the town. The town crier was sent to gather the people, and they received their melancholy message from the balcony of the church at Market Square. They could hardly comprehend what they heard.

Under the terms of the bill, the people were deprived of all choice in the election of governor and council. These men were henceforth to be appointed by His Majesty's Commission under the seal of Great Britain. This governor and, in his absence, the lieutenant governor, had the right to appoint judges of inferior courts and of the common pleas, the attorney general, all sheriffs, provosts, marshalls, etc. Upon vacancies among judges of the Supreme Court, the governor, without the consent of the council, could appoint judges of his own choice.

Townspeople could meet once a year to elect selectmen and other town officers, but no matters could be decided at that time. With the written permission of the governor, a special town meeting could be called to act on any other matter. Inhabitants were now denied the right to select jurymen; this prerogative was bestowed upon sheriffs only, who were beholden to the governor appointed by the king. Furthermore, upon the motion of either party involved, a cause or an action could be tried in any other county than where it was first brought.

The bill was to be enforced by the levying of fines or penalties, a gesture thought by the king to be very charitable under the existing circumstances. To Parliament, he confided, "Now, we have them."

None of the thirteen colonies could accept this Parliamentary Act. For communities like Newburyport which, up to this point in time, had proceeded cautiously and conservatively, it was the last straw. Hasty meetings were called while, for a time, no suggestion solidified into positive action. Then came an invitation from the Committee of Safety and Correspondence at Marblehead to a meeting to be attended by representatives from all communities of the county. With alacrity, leaders of Newburyport accepted this invitation. Sent to the meeting were: Tristram Dalton, Jonathan Jackson, Captain Jonathan Greenleaf, Stephen Cross and John Bromfield.

No member of the Sons of Liberty was chosen, not even Ezra Lunt.

The meeting was held in Ipswich because of its central location, and it lasted two days—September 6 and 7, 1774. It was quickly agreed that committees on safety and correspondence would be named in communities not now having one, and this included Newburyport. This was not the most important action to come out of the meeting. When the Newburyport delegates returned home, no time was lost.

Uppermost now in every man's mind, was separation from the mother country. They were dedicated to revolution, although no man liked to utter the dread word.

Openly and with determination, Newburyport's men prepared for war. Ground in the vicinity of Frog Pond, on the hill, was leveled for a training field for militia. The people went all out to prepare themselves and to provide themselves with arms and ammunition. Every male over sixteen years of age was required to appear for drill and gunnery practice. There was a choice of independent companies, or one could choose to join one of the existing companies belonging to the town. But all had to appear or answer to the selectmen with reasons for absenting themselves.

On September 23, 1774, a Committee of Safety and Correspondence was appointed by the town as follows:

| | |
|---|---|
| Hon. Benjamin Greenleaf | Capt. Jonathan Greenleaf |
| Patrick Tracy, Esq. | David Moody |
| Dr. John Sprague | Dr. Micajah Sawyer |
| William Atkins, Esq. | John Bromfield |
| Capt. James Hudson | John Stone |
| Edmund Bartlett | Maj. William Coffin |
| Ralph Cross, Jr. | Capt. Thomas Thomas |
| Tristram Dalton, Esq. | Capt. Joseph Huse |
| Edward Harris | Capt. Samuel Batchelor |
| Enoch Titcomb, Jr. | Moses Nowell |
| Capt. Jacob Boardman | Jonathan Jackson |
| William Teel | Richard Titcomb |
| Samuel Tufts | John Herbert |
| Capt. Moses Rogers | Moses Frazier |
| Jonathan Marsh | Capt. Nicholas Tracy |

## 4

## EZRA LUNT

The Newburyport Committee of Safety and Correspondence, in one of its first acts, set out to control the activities of the Sons of Liberty. Its intention was not to disband this unified group of patriots but, instead, to absorb its members into the ranks of the various militia. However, for the sake of security, it was necessary to dampen at once the phrenetic activities of some members. As was to be expected, the committee sent for Ezra Lunt.

This staunch supporter had the confidence of many conservatives. Sober and thoughtful by nature, it was a fortunate coincidence that he was at the time spokesman for the Sons of Liberty.

Ezra Lunt, together with a man named Tinges, was publisher of a local newspaper called *The Essex Journal and Merrimack Packet*. Using his paper, guarded writings had kept the people informed of the actions of the crown. Lunt had gone a step further in his already overburdened schedule.

In August of 1774, he began plying a stagecoach between Newburyport and Boston, traveling by way of Ipswich to Danvers, to Salem, and thence to Boston. He advertised in his newspaper that his stage, drawn by four horses for speed, would leave Newburyport and Boston on alternate days, making three round trips each week.

It was not Lunt's practice to drive the coach himself, but sometimes he did, and many an important person was spirited to and from meetings north of Boston. Many an important exchange of intelligence bridged the miles.

It is safe to assume that the British, through their native informers, soon learned that Ezra Lunt played a heavy role in the ranks of the opposition to the king. That being the case, it is not surprising that events, as they unfolded, led the Lunt family deeper and deeper into the mire of open revolt.

It was toward the end of September in the year 1774 that the Newburyport Committee of Safety and Correspondence summoned Ezra Lunt to meet with them. Ezra invited Henry, who was home between voyages to the Indies, to go along with him.

Taking the back streets and narrow alleys, Ezra and Henry visited two tap rooms before proceeding to the meeting at Jonathan Greenleaf's home on Water Street. As they moved at a seemingly aimless pace, Henry asked questions as to why the need for such subterfuge.

Ezra explained, "The time has come for the exercising of great caution, brother. While we meet with Jonathan Greenleaf and nine other members of the committee, the others will be having a soirée at the home of John Bromfield in the hope that it is there the Loyalists will look for any untoward activity and where the traitors will function."

Henry asked, "And the Sons of Liberty, what of their evening's work?"

Ezra replied, "Certain of them will watch and listen. The others will provide a drunken spectacle at Market Square and then follow the town crier all the way to John Bromfield's house, where they will knock on the doors and windows to bedevil the revelers."

Henry shook his head in bewilderment. It all sounded so much like child's play and well outside the boundaries of dignity and good taste. "No wonder," he thought, "that the British captains make mock of us and find us fair game." But to Ezra, he said nothing.

Nevertheless, the elder brother knew well what was going on in the mind of the younger. "Henry," he gently chided, "our very lives are now at stake. There's not a man among us but fears for his head. Yet, we cannot strike for independence at this time unless we are forced, because we are not ready. If playing the part of oafs and fools will gain us time—well then, this is the part we must play."

Soon they were at the Greenleaf home. Crossing a broad sill through a wide oak door, the brothers entered a darkened, broad hallway and were drawn into a big, square room toward the rear of the house. It was the dining room, and a group of ten men were tightly seated around the dining-room table. Their host, Mr. Greenleaf, who had met them at the door, bade them be seated.

Henry Lunt was certain that Ezra felt as awkward as he, placed as they were outside the circle and seated to one side in stiff, rush-bottom chairs while the others about the table enjoyed comfortable arm chairs with soft cushion seats.

There were more of these comfortable chairs about, and there was room to be made at the table. Henry felt the fire in his cheeks as he glanced about him in fierce resentment. He caught the eye of his kinsman, Enoch Titcomb, who sat with his back to them and seemed to leer over his shoulder.

Accustomed to the giving of orders, Henry had all he could do to remain quiet when he wanted nothing more than to demand that Titcomb, and all others who were showing their backs, turn and face them. Henry said silently to the clubbed heads and faces across the table, "I am as well born as you. I, at twenty-two years of age, captain your ships and order your men."

Henry rose to his feet and suddenly realized that Ezra, for once, stood with him. It seemed this meeting was never to start. Nor would it have but for the quick and sensitive reaction of its chairman, Mr. Tristram Dalton.* Mr. Dalton was on his feet and around the table with a speed none would have suspected possible from one of his weight and size. His dark-haired wig went slightly awry, that was all. He placed a hand on each brother's shoulder. "Come gentlemen," he said in a voice of pleasant resonance, as if no innuendo had been caught," you, being reasonable men and kin to some of us, come sit in with us."

Swiftly and smoothly, Mr. Dalton moved chairs about and made room at the table. Soon Ezra and Henry were shoulder to shoulder within the circle of men. Now, the business at hand could begin. It was not to be easy.

After some discussion of the times and their ills, a silence fell. Mr. Dalton, who had been covertly observing the reactions of the Lunt men, had decided that the time had come to attack the issue. "Now, Ezra," he said, "there is a matter most uncomfortable to seize upon, for there is a chance that you may

* See Appendix H.

misunderstand. However, the time has come when all men must choose their sides and choose them well. Some will do the planning, some will carry the orders, and some will do their bidding."

Mr. Dalton's words were directed at Ezra Lunt, whose reaction was calm and who made a courteous reply. "Sir," he said, "I presume you would like to discuss what shall be done to channel the activities of the Sons of Liberty."

Obviously, those present had not expected such a direct approach nor so calm a rejoinder. Glances were exchanged among some men at the table.

Henry's hackles again began to rise. "Oh, these patronizing merchants! For God's sake," he thought, "why don't they take to the subject like men ought. Were such as these an example of all planners of liberty?" He moved again as if to rise.

This time, Ezra put out his hand to bid his brother wait. Ezra was looking at Mr. Dalton. That gentleman, one of well-rounded education and excellent manners, struck the table with the flat of his hand commanding silence. His fingers then drummed the polished, brown surface. Suddenly, he was on his feet and again around the table. A word here and a gesture there and, all at once, the brothers found themselves at opposite sides of the table. Then, Mr. Dalton spoke rapidly and openly. "Now gentlemen," he said, "we must engage in serious talk. We live in critical times and can no longer afford to proceed on our ways separately. We will now, therefore, lend a respectful ear to Mr. Ezra Lunt."

Ezra spoke openly and honestly, calling for whatever resentments there might be against the activities of the Sons of Liberty to be declared right then. Talking then became easier, with Mr. Dalton always quick to apply soothing balm before it got out of hand.

Mr. Harris protested the harassment of suspected Tories. It seemed to Henry Lunt that the speaker's voice, which was high and thin, marred his argument. His protestations were not based on recent punishments as much as the defense of each man in his right of opinion.

Mr. David Moody warned that some people now feared the Sons of Liberty as much as they feared the English revenue officers. His remarks annoyed Henry the most of all. Ezra's response to this annoyed his brother even more.

Ezra replied, "I realize that this is the case, and I am sorry for it. But, I must point out that the majority of our members do not engage in rough or extreme activities, save where such are according to the basic plan."

Henry began to realize that his elder brother was more in accord with these merchant members of the Committee of Safety and Correspondence than he had heretofore thought possible. It seemed that events were moving fast on the home scene, and it was hard for one whose life was mainly at sea to adjust to these sudden changes.

Even as he pondered, Henry became aware that Mr. Tracy was now balancing the scale by pointing to atrocities against American seamen by British naval officers. The young captain was moved to speak, and he found himself most articulate as, with trembling voice, he told of Americans pressed into service in the British navy after being forcibly taken from their merchant ships. "Even masters," he said, "were being so treated. And those who will not serve, because they cannot, are thrown into prison aboard the man-of-war that would have them as crew."

Mr. Tracy answered him with soothing words. "Soon, we will oppose them at their own sport," he assured.

Henry cried, "What? A navy?"

Mr. Tracy smiled and reached for his snuff box. He nodded, looked about knowingly, and murmured, "Perhaps."

"So," thought Henry, "there is more than rumor to the tales I have been hearing." Aloud, he said, "Surely not privateers! Already we attract the scum of the earth to our waterfront by whispers going about of gainful rewards through the taking of prize ships as a retaliatory action by American merchantmen. Is this not piracy of a sort?"

Henry Lunt had touched a very sensitive nerve in the preparations for rebellion. Some of the gentlemen about the table, including Mr. Tracy, bristled. That gentleman had good reason for objection. His sizeable fortune, invested in the building of merchant ships and in trade, was at stake. (See Appendix A, p. 209.) Neither he nor others engaged in like occupations could afford to await the denouement. Heatedly, Mr. Tracy defended his position. While working and praying toward a decent Continental navy, they must make do with what they had, and the

Continental government would issue such commissions and papers as would make their actions legal.

"The way it is seen," Mr. Tracy declared, "is that privateers will provide staying action while protecting our assets."

Henry Lunt could not believe what he was hearing. It was all very well and good for these merchants to sit at home and plan their strategy while the men who sailed their ships took all the risk. To pit a merchantman against a British man-of-war was unthinkable. He spoke his mind.

"If we are to fight on water, let it be from ships built for war, properly commissioned and manned by men who are trained for war. Let us not go forth in made-over merchantmen built for cargo and not for guns." He asked bitterly, "Are we to appear as fools before the great navy of the mistress of the seas?"

His words were admittedly the words of a bold, young man, brave with the untried bravery of youth. He told himself, but not those present, "Never will I go in a privateer for Nathaniel Tracy." Nor did he; but two years later he ate his words and went on a privateer anyway.

Henry Lunt went out on the privateer *Dalton*, sponsored by Tristram Dalton and others. But that was after the fiasco of the Rhode Island navy. After his captain, John Paul Jones, was left chafing for a decent commission, and after his brother, Daniel Lunt, was taken from off a merchant ship by the British.

Henry, at last, had nearly broken up the meeting at hand. He would have done so had Ezra not offered him a stern reprimand, thereby, by right of seniority, putting the bit to his teeth. Appealing for tolerance of his brother's impetuous advances, Ezra made further apology for the Sons of Liberty and promised a cooling of tempers all around. "We will all," he assured, looking darkly at Henry, "change to meet the times. We will unite as men should for the common good."

Mr. Dalton, who had risen and now stood at the sideboard with their host, Jonathan Greenleaf, raised a glass inviting all to join him. Glasses were raised high in toast after toast as the meeting drew leisurely to a close. Feeling as chastized as a pink-cheeked boy, Henry nevertheless drank punch laced with rum with the gusto of a man. A little later, he and Ezra departed.

The Lunt brothers spoke little as they took their way home by the back streets. Two red-coated British soldiers had them halt as they entered Crumb Alley but let them pass without protest as soon as they were identified.

Henry thought, "was ever a condition more strange?" It was certain that many Americans involved in rebellion were well known to the British. Yet, they took no open action against them. Again, the lion had underestimated the strength of the mouse.

They were resolute that night, the brothers Lunt, as they walked shoulder to shoulder through the pitch blackness. It was perhaps as well that they could not foresee what lay ahead, when Ezra would fight on land and Henry on the sea. But Henry's would be the more telling experience, for he would bask in the reflected glory of John Paul Jones, the first American captain to capture a British man-of-war.

5

## CRY OF DEFIANCE

Word that the British were marching on Lexington reached Newburyport on April 18, 1775. Receiving the message at the Putnam house in Danvers, where his stagecoach had halted en route to Boston, Ezra Lunt borrowed a fleet pony and galloped him all the way. He thundered into Market Square in Newburyport at supper time followed by horsemen gathered along the way from the Newbury Lower Green and from Rowley.

Amid an atmosphere of confusion and panic, the Minute Men were called up. Women wept and children cowered in their beds as hasty preparations went forward.

By eleven o'clock in the dark of night, they shouldered their muskets and marched from town in ragged ranks. In groups of three to five they slipped through the night like fugitives fleeing from justice rather than free men in the pursuit of liberty. Fleet of foot, they ran like Indians, short-cutting the hills for the valleys. Not until Bunker Hill would these northeast patriots draw up in orderly ranks to face the precisely trained British regulars.

Their thoughts were morbid and fearful, for at the time of their departure from Newburyport, rumor had it strongly that the king's soldiers had set the town of Ipswich on fire.

The Minute Men of Newburyport wasted their energies in their hasty rallying to aid their compatriots at Lexington and at Concord. By the time they had reached Danvers, the skirmish was over, and the British had withdrawn their ranks to their barracks in Boston and aboard the *Somerset,* a man-of-war swinging sullenly at her moorings off Charlestown Bay.

The British officers were in closet to make an uneasy debriefing of their night's work, which had gained them little. Something had gone wrong with the plan to take the Americans by surprise and seize their store of ammunition. They counted their dead and wounded and discovered for the first time that they had no cause for rejoicing.

Newburyport had suffered under acts of the crown as much as any other seacoast community and even more than many. Yet, she had been one of those most reluctant to declare for independence from the mother country. Now, her cry of defiance could be heard as loud and as long as any. By late spring of the year 1775, every man capable of carrying arms, including sixteen year olds, was enrolled and meeting for military practice. Younger boys and old men (over forty) held their separate drills as guardians of the home front and were the new "Sons of Liberty."

When war was first anticipated at the initial meeting of the Continental Congress, Newburyport sent a representative to suggest conciliatory measures, due to all that the town had at stake in commerce and trade. This was in the year 1774 when the die had already been cast, and the attitude of the Newburyport representative was not received with favor. In fact, several of the gentlemen present at the first Continental Congress, from then on, were inclined to look with disfavor and suspicion on anyone from this community.

The assumption that Newburyport was a Tory Town was an unfair one. Once the decision was made for separation from England, once the tremulous idea had become accustomed to, Newburyport townsmen neither flinched nor shirked. In May, 1775, they drew a resolution in a full town meeting resolving that, "If the Honorable Continental Congress should, for the safety of the United Colonies, declare themselves independent of the Kingdom of Great Britain, this town will with its lives and fortunes support it in measure...."

The Revolutionary War was more than a decade in the making when the British marched out from Boston to seize the military stores of the Americans at Concord. It was a shorter march to Charlestown, where larger stores were concealed, had their intelligence sent them there.

The British regulars set out in the dark of night and marched in well ordered ranks to the beat of muffled drums, which nevertheless were noisy enough to awaken a countryside. It was a fine spring day on April 19 when they marched up to Lexington. All that was required, so they thought, was a showing of strength and the taking of a few prisoners.

The Americans, with the memory of the Boston massacre still festering in their hearts and minds, had other ideas and regarded the action as open warfare. A front line defense of seventy Americans greeted the astounded British at Lexington and stopped them in a holding action long enough for Minute Men to muster at Concord. In the exchange of shot, four Americans were killed and nine were wounded before the British pressed on to their humiliating encounter at Concord.

The fires of revolution were permanently ignited on that day when the American freemen introduced the tactics of the Indian fighter to the British tacticians. The red-coated British regulars, in orderly march, made perfect targets for the straight-shooting colonials from places of concealment behind trees and stone walls. The perfect advance of soldiers in lines fell back and broke away. Soon the British were retreating in frantic disorder.

The next major encounter between the two forces would be at Bunker Hill, where the British would suffer another put-down at the hands of the indomitable colonists. Had the Americans not run out of ammunition, they would have won this battle in which they are credited with killing nearly one thousand of the enemy. This recorded figure was probably exaggerated, but the facts were not. The only trouble was, the war was just beginning.

There was to be a battle at Bunker Hill, and a breastwork was being thrown up there in invitation to the British grenadiers.

Back in Newburyport, Ezra Lunt was measuring the weight of his patriotism against his thirty-two years of hard work for security in his old age. Some of his kinsmen had gone on the march to Concord with the company of Newburyport Minute Men, but Ezra had not gone, in keeping with the assignment of watch dog he had hitherto been required to maintain.

Ezra's decision was not, after all, hard coming. He knew he could no longer remain on the sidelines of actual combat. He resolved to take steps at once to replace the company of Minute Men, still out on the road to Concord, with a new one to act in "defense of the town."

It was while attending a special church service that Ezra Lunt reached his decision to go all the way with revolution. The

Reverend Jonathan Parsons, ailing pastor of the Old South Presbyterian church who was whipped to a fiery discourse by events at Lexington and Concord, went from a sick bed to his church on Monday, April 25. There, in the high pulpit, looking down upon his full congregation, he delivered the emotional sermon of his life. The good parson was so weak he could hardly stand and had to be supported, but his voice, although trembling, was loud as he charged every man who loved home and country to do his duty. They must, he commanded, discount all personal loss or gain to take up arms in defense of God and country.

Ezra Lunt felt each word was a flaming dagger held to his heart as he sat with his silently weeping wife and family in their ancient box pew. Ezra had spent long hours prior to this in self-examination and was therefore primed to an heroic and spectacular performance. There, in his church, before his family, friends, and neighbors, he made his own declaration of war.

On April 25, 1775, in Old South Church, Newburyport, Ezra Lunt arose to his feet, following the exhortation by the Reverend Jonathan Parsons, and moved to the broad aisle of the church. There, he formed a revolutionary company.*

Bidding all brave men, who would, to follow him, Lunt, stern of countenance, moved with measured tread to the out of doors and thence to the drill field at Frog Pond. At least twelve men followed him, and as they marched along, more men and boys fell in. Thus, could Ezra himself, inspire men to follow his leadership, and follow him they would all the way to Bunker Hill and Valley Forge.

On the first day of May, Ezra Lunt did two things. First, he sold his interest in the local newspaper, *The Essex Journal and Merrimack Packet*, to John Mycall, a school master, of Amesbury town, located up the Merrimack River going west. Second, he formally enlisted in the Revolutionary Army.

There were twenty-two men in the military company of Major Ezra Lunt, formed officially on May 2, 1775. Officers were chosen on Monday, May 8, when Paul Lunt, Ezra's cousin, recently home from the march to Concord, was named a first lieutenant. The company, completed, left Newburyport on May

* See Appendix G.

10, marching by way of Rowley, Ipswich, and Danvers to Cambridge, where ranks were forming for the Battle of Bunker Hill. By the time of departure, their ranks had swelled to sixty men.

The company set out from Newburyport with the cheers of townsmen ringing in their ears. They were met by both cheers and jeers as they moved along, and families came out of doors as dwellings were passed by. As they marched through the open countryside, the ranks relaxed to a leisurely pace while runners and scouts on ahead kept the watch. Ezra and Paul Lunt then marched together, but it was not until they reached Rowley that they had time in the pause for refreshment, to speak together. Paul then related some of his experiences while on the road to Concord, and the difficulties encountered as the Minute Men worked their way back to Newburyport. Paul also expressed a personal worry for his wife, who, in a few months time, would give birth to a child.

The Ezra Lunt company paused at Ipswich on the evening of Wednesday, May 10, for an over night, and, routing out at crack of dawn, they marched to Putnam's at Danvers for breakfast. Following a sermon by the Reverend Hitchcock, who preached from the Psalms, they pressed on. They arrived at Cambridge on Friday, May 12, where they stopped at John Bolin's house for refreshments. Then they marched to Steadman's where they were quartered.

The men settled down to army life with difficulty, but routine drills and false alerts were almost constant. A commotion during one night provided embarrassment for Ezra when a bad woman was discovered in the quarters of his company. She was drummed from camp, and her companion in sin was locked in a dark hole for a day.

Ezra Lunt was very much disappointed in his role at Bunker Hill when his company was assigned to back-up action and scouting the enemy. The battle took place on June 17, 1775, and Major Ezra Lunt's militia did, after all, receive special commendation. When, their ammunition used up, the Americans were forced to retreat, Lunt and his Newburyport company held off the British at the rear of that retreat, thereby cutting down casualties. Several of their number were wounded.

The military company of Ezra Lunt was active from May to

the end of December, 1775, but many faces changed. Enlistments were only for three months at a time, and that was all to which the men could be held. Some mustered out in September to join with General Benedict Arnold's expedition to Quebec, sailing first from Newburyport to Kennebec. Others just went home. But Paul Lunt stayed with Ezra most loyally until the company was disbanded.

Ezra Lunt's company disbanded in December, the prospects of further privation in the dead of winter an impossibility. They straggled back home a few at a time, and Ezra, remembering the impending birth of a child, insisted that his cousin Paul go on ahead. Traveling in the company of Samuel Noyes, Paul arrived at the Noyes home in Newbury on December 23 at seven o'clock in the evening. There, he rested for a time. At nine o'clock he arrived at his own house and found his wife in the process of giving birth. Their first son, named Joshua Coffin Lunt, was born one hour later. It made Paul Lunt feel that his sacrifice had been worth while. His joy was to change to sorrow.

The long months of worry and overwork had taken their toll of his wife, and she lay weak and ill for days, unable to nurse her child. The tiny boy died ten days later, and his grieving father later confided to his cousin, Ezra, "He lived ten days and departed this evil world."

6

## HENRY LUNT MARRIES

They were nearing the shores of home, and Captain Henry Lunt was up in the yards again. This dare-devil mariner, so cautious with the life of his ship, seemed at times to have no regard for his own life, but it was this characteristic which made him most popular with his crew. Lunt, they would admit, could outpractice them all, and he liked to prove it. Quick as a cat when dancing the ropes, he could beat them all to the top of the ship, laughing down at all contenders from the flirting, gigantic sails. Oft times, then, he would jam a tarpaulin hat on his clubbed, blonde head and do a fair hornpipe to his peril along a spar. He had earned the right to the name of captain, but he was the perfect prototype of the second mate, a role later selected for him by that shrewd connoisseur of men, John Paul Jones.

The second mate in sailing ships had what was called—and rightly—a dog's berth. Never quite set apart, as his title implied, he was liaison between the captain and crew. He was required to go aloft and to be on deck most of the time. Although he was quartered in the cabin of the ship, he most usually ate alone the lustreless rations of second serving. He was responsible for all supplies relating to the ship's maintenance and repair, and he was expected to know the exact location where the smallest part was stored. He was, in short, expected to maintain the dignity, and command the respect, of an officer while working at the level of the able seaman.

The second mate was traditionally a dour person with deeply harbored resentments. He despised his immediate superior, the master's mate, and regarded him as a self-seeking tattle-tale.

In the days of sailing ships, an elevation to the rank of second mate was the real test of seamanship, and it was supposed to separate the men from the boys. By this yardstick did his fellows judge him, and if they judged him well, he was worthy to go on to become master of a ship. Henry Lunt of Newbury, Massachusetts, had long since passed the test with colors flying, and thus, when his call came, he was ready for an historic role at sea in the American Revolution.

Henry Lunt had reason for exuberance as he sighted what seemed to be the friendly outline of the shores of home in that month of June, 1775. He was home to marry Sarah, the bride he had longed to take for the best part of three years gone. Henry had confided to his family, "Love of woman have I known, but none have I loved before my own Sarah Orcutt. Her I will wed or wed no other."

The captain's mood had impregnated that of his entire crew. They seemed to have had a charmed voyage on this particular run from the Indies. Their merchantman had outrun two heavy, British naval vessels, one just south of Boston, and skillful seamanship had done it. With full sails set, they had darted like an arrow with sails almost raking the sea.

As they came within sight of Ipswich Bay, they encountered a disappointment and were forced to anchor off the north Plum Island reef within sound of the church bells of home. The island shore, verdant with pine and white with plum-bush blossoms, tantalized sailors hungry for home and for dearly loved faces. They knew they had been sighted from the Newburyport rooftops. They could hear the rhythmic clanging of the church bells, and this could mean only one thing. They were being warned of a hidden danger. Caution was now necessary. They drew in their sails and settled to wait. It was well that they did this. In back of the dunes and out of their sight was an encampment of British regulars. On the other side, a small boat put out to them by slow degrees. In it were Captain Offin Boardman, Captain Benjamin Lunt, a kinsman of Henry, and Captain David Coates.

After a hearty welcome to the homecomers, important information was given to them, and they were warned of the wooden piers recently put down in the Merrimack River channel near the black rocks. They had been put there to prevent vessels from passing freely in and out of the Newburyport harbor without first being examined.

The three captains stayed aboard to await the fall of night to guide them in. The British sent sentinels to the tops of the dunes to observe their activities, but on this occasion, they made no attempt to board their ship.

Privately, Henry Lunt questioned the wisdom of sinking piers in the river. He regarded the harbor, with its treacherous currents and hidden shoals, challenge enough for either friend or foe. But there was no time for dwelling upon such pros or cons; there was other news of greater impact. Captain Boardman had news to knock all other from Captain Lunt's head, even thoughts of his impending marriage. For the first time he learned of the violent happenings at Lexington and Concord.

Henry cried out in anger, "Now, by God, here is injustice and murder before all the world."

The old captain made fierce reply, "It is more than all that, son. It is war!"

Hitherto, Henry had been reluctant to accept war as the inevitable solution, influenced as he was by the conservative Newburyport community. All he had ever wanted was to sail before the mast in hurry-up trips to the Indies; to pit his strength against his best known adversary—the sea; to sail far and come home with a full sum of cargo; then, to walk the hard earth with Sarah on his arm with the greeting of kinfolk and friends sweet in his ears.

This was Henry Lunt's dream, and he thought again of Sarah. A lump came into his throat. Sarah's people were of the land and real pacifists in their beliefs. Henry was remembering one day a year before when he and Sarah, accompanied by her father, John Orcutt, wandered through the Newburyport market place. Henry had ridden with them in their farm wagon from their West Newbury home, located west of Newburyport. It was week's end, and wagons moved with them fairly crowding the road the nearer they came to town.

The activities of the market spilled over into adjacent, wide streets, extending for a third of a mile along Water Street and the river front. There were people aplenty, staggering under the weight of goods being exchanged one to the other. Few there were with the hard cash to buy, but this did not particularly matter. Goods for exchange were really all one needed. Calico cloth, molasses, sugar, and East India spices attracted the country folk, but most of all, they bargained for salt and nails, items dearly needed which they were not permitted to manufacture by order of the king.

Due to the courtship of Sarah by Henry, the Orcutts remained overnight with the Lunt family. Courtesy then required that Henry accompany them to church in Market Square on Sunday. He did not like the theology of that church.

Henry, fidgety and angry by turns, felt the pressure of Sarah's hand on his arm in mute appeal. So he listened, for her sake, to a sermon of great length, both morning and afternoon. Silently, red of face, he writhed hearing words that exhorted him to be controlled and led by the clergy who would bring him back to the fold, subsurvient once more to Britain. He could not return directly the glances of either Sarah or her parents and was glad to send them homeward at late afternoon after riding with them to the edge of Newburyport. Almost, but not quite, he thought to end his suit after Sarah. Realizing he could never do this, he forgave her parents their religious affiliation and decided that they were not to blame. How could they be when ministers of the Lord engaged in infantile meanderings of the spirit with no apparent knowledge of the real state of affairs.

On that June morning of his return home, after learning of Lexington and Concord, Henry took the yoke of revolution on his shoulders. But first, he must see Sarah and plan their immediate wedding. He mounted his horse and rode west along the river to the Orcutt home.

Henry Lunt was not well received by the Orcutts. They met him in the forward parlor, which caused his heart to sink at such a formality. Mr. and Mrs. Orcutt sat stiffly side by side, nor did Mr. Orcutt rise to greet his potential son-in-law.

The parlor had the unpleasant odor of musk, as does a room closed up and infrequently used. Henry's heart sank even lower, but he would not give up hope. His eyes fixed feverishly on the door to the middle hallway where green velvet portieres hung without motion. So eager was he for the sight of Sarah and the sound of her rich, full-timbred voice, he cared not that her parents were watching him closely.

Sarah did not appear.

Mr. Orcutt then spoke of other things. He talked of horses and their manners, a subject of which he was most inordinately fond. He spoke of the trials of running a large plantation.

Mrs. Orcutt interrupted whenever she could, darting in like a sparrow intent on picking and prying. Alternately, she deplored the life of a mariner's wife and sniffled into her handkerchief. She vowed that her daughter should not give her life to work and loneliness and be the wife of an errant sailor. Mrs. Orcutt, a pretty faced woman and delicately plump, had a life far removed from that of a poor farmer and knew little of the life of a sailor's wife. She had a goodly number of servants and slaves, both white and black, who waited on her hand and foot. She had always, before, been very kind to Henry.

On this occasion, she was nervously stuffing her nostrils and underlip with snuff, to stem, she said, an ague. She brushed aside Henry's offered condolences. At length, the poor lady, overcome with embarrassment, became quite tipsy and ordered tea. She then staggered about, pouring the tea the maid servant brought anywhere but in the teacups. She finally burst into loud sobbing, tore the mop cap from her head, and covered her face with it. She lunged from their sights not to return.

Wanting to laugh, which he dared not do, while at the point of bursting with anger, Henry Lunt begged permission of Mr. Orcutt to withdraw. But that gentleman was not through, and he waved the other man down. His wife's ridiculous performance he ignored.

"Now, Henry," he said, "let us talk as men, and friends, too, I hope. Let us, in a word, be practical."

Having been there an hour without sight or sign of his espoused wife, this was too much. "How, sir, can we talk?" inquired the younger man through clenched teeth.

Mr. Orcutt arose and moved to a brown, wood secretary across the room. He paced up and down before it, frowning. He went to the fireplace and leaned one arm on its narrow, white mantel. A tall clock in the corner with a steep cathedral spire banged the hour loudly.

Suddenly, just when he thought he could endure no more, Henry had a strong sense of someone listening in the hall, and he thought he detected movement in the portieres. It was indeed

Sarah, and he suspected it was, this was not the auspicious moment for her to appear.

Nor did she.

Her father had the frames of small spectacles, like those favored by Ben Franklin, perched low on his nose and looped to his ears. He picked up to read what looked like, and, indeed, proved to be, a letter.

He shook the letter importantly. "Henry," he said, "I have here a letter from England, and I want you to heed well its contents which I shall read to you, for upon your reaction depends your very future."

Henry caught his meaning as his heart sank further. Could this mean that they were on opposite sides? Was this the end of his chances with Sarah? Although he felt compelled to cry out, Henry found instead the composure to wait and listen. The gist of the letter as read by Mr. Orcutt was ominous.

> The colonists will fail. They are not able to raise enough sheep to supply them wool. The attempt within these thirty-five years in the making of nails always miscarries because they can be imported from England much cheaper.
>
> People do not go into the manufacture of their needs because every man, for a mere bagatelle, can avail himself of 200 acres of land with which he can support himself and his family more easily than by going into manufacturing.
>
> It follows, of course, by the American plan of importation they will, in two years time, not have enough clothes to protect them against the severity of weather, nor nails to build homes.
>
> If their ports are kept well blocked, they will be denied what have become necessities of life to them, such as molasses, coffee, cocoa, sugar, rum, etc., with no other drink but water and a little ordinary cider from October to June.
>
> The people of the seaport towns of New England live on salt provisions more than three quarters of the year, and the stoppage of salt alone will provide their ruin.

A large army ravaging the country will put a stop to agriculture.

If they war, I give them two years. . . .

When Mr. Orcutt had finished reading, he removed his glasses and dangled them from one hand as he moved grandly about the room. He shook the letter under Henry Lunt's nose.

His attitude, Henry thought, was as a triumphant gladiator who had delivered the coup de grace. Feeling betrayed, the younger man drew himself up to his full height and squared his shoulders. He would have no more talk of a traitorous nature. What his stormy countenance revealed, he dared not contemplate.

Henry Lunt was wearing the dark waistcoat and buff-colored britches soon to be his only uniform in the Continental navy, but never would he feel more like a fighting marine than at that moment of confrontation with his potential father-in-law. What he projected he could not tell, but it seemed to take the wind out of the older man's sails.

Slowly, much to Henry's amazement, Mr. Orcutt blew down before him and staggered a bit as he sank into a convenient chair. It occurred to Henry that he had been expected to betray himself with hot-headed protestations ere this. He had actually won this skirmish, no doubt one of many being held in many a household, presaging the events to come.

Wisely, the young man did not press his advantage, and bowing his head respectfully, he withdrew without one bitter exchange of words having taken place. This was a discipline to be respected, and one to uphold the dignity of the man, Henry Lunt, through later and even more trying times.

The Orcutt's black boy, Julius, with whom Henry had a friendly relationship, patted his shoulder as he brought his horse into the tree-shaded yard. Henry nodded his thanks and acknowledged his greeting but was too disconsolate to engage in conversation. Because of this, he also missed the knowing twinkle in Julius's dark eyes. He mounted his horse and started stiffly down the lane. And then, he heard the miracle of a familiar trill behind him. He wheeled his horse.

Sarah, running full skirted, her black hair unbound and blowing in the wind, caught up with him as he charged to meet her. Henry swung his bride up behind him, where she rode astride like a witch and hugged herself to him tightly. Julius laughed heartily behind, and Henry Lunt yelled lustily into the high arch of the bright blue sky as they streaked away over the greening earth.

Sarah went home with Henry where she remained for three days before her father capitulated. The marriage took place, as planned, the following Sunday in the same musty-smelling front parlor where Henry had struggled and fought for his wife.

Three months later, leaving Sarah at his father's home in Newbury, Henry Lunt was on his way to Philadelphia and a rendezvous with John Paul Jones in the Rhode Island navy.

## 7

## THE TAVERN MEETING

John Paul Jones was an able judge of men in his ability to pick and choose those most likely to help him to succeed. One of these, a gentleman from North Carolina, lived almost on his doorstep.

Joseph Hewes, a champion of Jones from beginning to end, was one of the signers of the Declaration of Independence and otherwise so dedicated to the cause of American independence that he gave up his religion in the Society of Friends because he had departed from its attitude of pacifism. In 1774, Hewes was sent from Edenton (sometimes called Roanoke) to the Congress at Philadelphia, and he served there until he died on November 10, 1779.

John Paul Jones, long before this, had struck up an almost daily relationship with Hewes, and their common interest was the formation of an American navy, which they deemed essential for the protection of the American coastline.

When Hewes left Fredricksburg for the seat of the new government at Philadelphia, Jones was not far behind him, for the time was momentous for all those who sought commissions. There could be no doubt that Congress was of the same mind as the men from Virginia, as was demonstrated by one of its first acts.

A committee was appointed to outfit armed vessels, and appointed to this committee were Joseph Hewes, John Hancock, William Whipple, Francis Hopkins, George Read, George Walton, Arthur Middleton, Francis Lewis and Robert Morris. In addition to Hewes, Morris and Whipple could be counted on by John Paul Jones to further his cause. He engaged in almost constant correspondence and meetings with all three of these gentlemen.

Jones proved more ready for the new navy than it was for him. There were powerful interests at work from the northeast seacoast communities, particularly Rhode Island. Farther north, at Newburyport, Portsmouth, Marblehead, Salem, Gloucester, and even Boston, supplies were plentiful, and ships and cannon were being built. But the robust Yankees were not strong on drawingroom politics, nor were they as close to the government seat as those more familiar with political action. The Rhode Island contingent was closer, better represented, and first on deck.

Contentious debating consumed endless hours, days, and weeks, for men were wordy in those days. John Paul Jones fumed and fussed after a commission, while Joseph Hewes and Robert Morris did their best to placate him with promises of their full support. But when all was cut and dried, their efforts stood for little.

There could be no doubt that Jones, with his background and record of British naval service, was the best potential officer on the scene. Nevertheless, it soon became evident that his appointment was being circumvented because the balance of power on the Marine Committee tipped in another direction.

Jones had arrived in Philadelphia from Virginia by way of the Virginia gentry, not even from a seaboard community. Few persons had time to read dossiers in those days. It was oratory and power all the way. Jones would have to prove himself the hard way, and he wisely accepted the fact. When it was brought home to him that he was not to captain a ship in the new navy, he swallowed his disappointment and set his sights on a lesser berth, one from which he could work and attract attention. He began to harp at his friends, extolling his abilities as lieutenant in charge of a gun deck.

Receipt of news that two transports, armed and carrying military supplies for the British, were en route from Quebec, forced Congress into action. On October 5, 1775, a small committee, consisting of Silas Deane of Connecticut, John Langdon of New Hampshire, and Stephen Gadsden of South Carolina, was appointed. Acting in haste, this committee, on the same day, reported back to Congress, with the result that George Washington was ordered to borrow two cruisers belonging to Massachusetts.

Two days before this, in private caucus, the Rhode Island delegation, not to be outdone, voted for broader action. They drew up a plan for the formation of a fleet for national defense, and they were successful in bringing this before Congress on October 7. A debate ensued, led by the Honorable Stephen Hopkins, long time governor of Rhode Island. In cahoots with him outside his own delegation, were some strong figures. These included, Silas Deane, afterwards commissioner to France for a time, John Rutledge, Christopher Gadsden, the Reverend Dr. Abbly of Georgia, and John Adams of Massachusetts.

Most frustrating for those who had worked long and hard to bring order out of chaos was the result of that day-long debate, for it only brought about further delay. The decision to borrow ships from Massachusetts was changed to a "looking into the purchase of warships for the government." The government being penniless, this was looked upon by the minority as foolish.

Bitter words of reproof and contention were followed by more maneuvering behind the scenes. Then, surprisingly, there was action. On October 13, Congress passed a resolution ordering the immediate purchase of two sailing vessels, one of ten and one of fourteen guns to cruise eastward together for the purpose of intercepting the English forces in Boston. The *Lexington* and the *Reprisal* were designated, and the gentlemen would pay for these out of their own private pockets.

On October 30, this plan was advanced. The Marine Committee was increased to include John Adams, Stephen Hopkins, Joseph Hewes, and Richard Henry Lee. (The first committee was from then on ignored for a while.) Two large ships of thirty-six and twenty guns were added, their names being the *Alfred* and the *Columbus*.

On December 13, Congress increased the navy by thirteen more ships, again increased the Marine Committee, now referred to as the Naval Committee, and ordered a member from each colony.

Philadelphia, by this time, was teeming with ambitious candidates seeking commissions. John Paul Jones still stayed in a good, but by no means superior, position despite his strong supporters at the top.

The northeast contingent was to emerge the victor in the scramble. The lion's share of appointment-plums, due to the influence of its powerful, long-time governor, Stephen Hopkins, went to Rhode Island. He was also a kinsman of John Adams of Massachusetts.

John Paul Jones was among those bitterly disappointed when it was announced that Esek Hopkins, brother of Stephen, was to be commander-in-chief. John, however, fared better than Henry Lunt and others. The officers were named as follows: Abraham Whipple, related to the Hopkins family, received command of the *Columbus*; John B. Hopkins, son of Esek, would command the *Cabot*; Nicholas Biddle, captain of the *Andrea Doria*, represented the wealthy of Philadelphia; Dudley Saltonstall of Massachusetts became captain of the *Alfred*.

Joseph Hewes had succeeded in placing John Paul Jones among the first lieutenants. In spite of the fact that Hewes was entrusted with the practical work of organizing and equipping the fleet, due to his experience as a ship owner, he was allowed only one appointment to the list of ships' officers. He promptly named Jones, who was forever grateful.

The *Alfred* was the largest of the four vessels purchased by the Continental Congress Naval Committee. It was therefore designated as the flagship of the new fleet. John Paul Jones, assigned to the *Alfred*, was given charge of the lower gun deck. The time it took for all of this to happen posed an immediate problem for Jones, who, up to now, seemed to be one of the few who knew what he was doing.

Nevertheless, the scramble for the best men was on, with those officers appointed early grabbing up the known able seamen. By the time John Paul Jones had his commission, many of the skilled mariners from merchant ships had been taken or had turned their faces toward home. A rumor that those not assigned to the ships would be automatically absorbed into the army had hastened their departures.

Jones was fretful but not fazed. He wanted men who could handle ships and take orders, preferably young men. He would teach them the techniques of war at sea, and he would teach them his way. He was conceited enough to be glad that the Americans as a whole knew very little concerning this. The lieutenant knew that his assignment was one he could handle well, and he intended to stand head and shoulders above the rest. Jones did not leave the ground work to others, nor did he hurry to sign up more men than he needed, as some were doing in order to fatten the army roles. He went to work at once to find his own crew at the Philadelphia waterfront.

Henry Lunt, true to his word, had come to Philadelphia among the first. He had sought out the Massachusetts delegation of the Naval Committee with high hopes, thinking that the letters of recommendation he carried from leading Newburyport mercantile and political figures would gain him a post suitable to his captain's rating. He was soon to learn that this was not the way the tide was moving. He was unable to gain audiences with any of his mentors; in fact, he could hardly wade through the numbers of men waiting in ante rooms. Finally, he sent his credentials in, although reluctant to let them out of his hands. His fears were well founded. He never did get to see anyone of consequence, and he never got his letters back. He was ready to give up in discouragement, especially when he began to hear on all sides that commissions must be purchased to raise money for the Continental treasury. He was more than ready to go to war for his country, but with a wife to support he had no money to give away.

It was early January, 1776, and the ships were about ready for outfitting. Near panic had set in among those seeking an able crew, and masters and mates were scurrying about, scooping up men like fish in a basket. Those from New England were in high demand and had no need to sell their wares, so well known were they throughout the colonies. But of commissions they received not an offer.

The Newburyport men of lower rank had all been taken or had set out for home. Henry Lunt was taking what would probably have been his last stroll along the Philadelphia waterfront when he heard an old shipmate hail him. It was Thomas Chase from Holmes Hole on Martha's Vineyard. Lunt, with several others, had wandered into a tavern to have some supper. He returned Chase's greeting quite heartily and was gratified when the other called, a smile creasing the leather of his face, "Captain Lunt, make your proper roll and bring your lads this way."

The men Henry Lunt had with him were not his lads, but, with good nature, he did as Chase had bidden. As they took their places at the benches around the tavern table, the island man turned to another half hidden in the shadows and murmured, "Now, sir, I have brought you the best."

Low as the words were spoken, Henry knew they referred to him and he was gratified indeed. At that moment, nothing more was said as they began eating and bumping mugs of brew in the conviviality of all seamen. But all through the supping, Henry was aware of inner excitement and of the man who sat half hidden in the shadow, who neither ate nor drank but constantly observed.

Lunt soon noticed that Thomas Chase seldom took his eyes from the hidden stranger who had not yet been introduced. Thomas, who had been a leader of the boisterous railery, became suddenly quiet, as if by a signal. There was a stillness at the table.

Then Chase looked directly at Henry Lunt, and he asked, "Have ye signed with one of the navy ships?"

"Nay," the Newbury man curtly replied. That he was feeling bitter was plain to see, for Henry could never hide his emotions. When Chase then directly asked him if he would consider signing for the gun deck of the *Alfred*, he hesitated while thinking, "I suppose I should first offer my thanks for my only offer to date." He did not say this aloud.

What he did say through tight lips was, "Not having a mentor in high places, I suppose I could forget my rank and become a powder monkey."

There was commotion as a bench moved back, and the man in shadows came suddenly alive. A voice like velvet cast in iron stung Henry Lunt to the quick. "A good and dutiful powder monkey you shall not be under me, for I intend to go in harm's way!"

Thomas Chase receded and became the shadow as the speaker took his place.

Here was John Paul Jones!

Henry Lunt would never forget that first meeting nor the sensation of dumb surprise that swept over him. It was as if he stood before a mirror. They looked so much alike, the two of them, that each recognized the fact at once—even with Henry in his homespun and Jones in his elegant uniform with ruffles at throat and wrists.

The lieutenant's words of reprimand, so softly spoken were a new approach, and Lunt stiffened for the tirade to come, but it did not follow. Instead, Jones turned to the business uppermost in his mind, and he encouraged Henry to speak and give a report of himself.

Henry Lunt said, "I must tell you, sir, that I have no letters of recommendation, for I turned them in at John Hancock's door, and there they were lost." Then, gathering the courage of indignation, he spilled it all out, telling of his training background, his rank, and his stake in the India trade. He brought forth something of a smile when he told of his resentment against politicians of the northeast.

Lieutenant Jones heard him out, gestured toward Chase, and then said, "But, yes." Then, he added, as if talking only to himself, "This is an ideal meeting, for every man of destiny should have a twin at hand, if only for a stand-in. You, sir, shall learn to imitate my every move. Only, you still shall not be me." Legs wide apart, hands tucked behind and under his waistcoat, Jones inspected Lunt from top to bottom.

The two did look enough alike to be twins. About the same height, five feet eight inches tall; each had a well proportioned body with sturdy legs and a face of regular features with determined chin. The differences were in the genes—Henry Lunt, half Dane and John Paul Jones half or wholly Scottish. Henry's hair was blonde while Jones's was sandy. Henry's eyes were azure blue; Jones' eyes were chameleon, sometimes gray, sometimes green, reminding the mariner of the changing moods of the sea.

From the time they were all together on the *Alfred*, Richard Dale, the dashing young first officer, was always heard to warn, "To know the way the keel lies, keep your eyes on the captain's eyes."

# 8

## *GLASGOW* ENCOUNTER

The new Continental navy fleet sailed from Philadelphia amid great ceremony on a cold, winter day. Henry Lunt was an able seaman on the flagship *Alfred* that would carry the commodore.

The young Lieutenant John Paul Jones stood in front at the rail, and the eyes of his men were as much on him as they were on the ceremony going on about them. They could not but remark that the lieutenant was dressed like a dandy in ruffles and braid and sword by his side.

"Still," said Henry Lunt in an aside to Thomas Chase, "I cannot blame him for his pretensions, for he plays a part in this affair that all might like to play." Jones was to raise the flag to the *Alfred*'s masthead at the proper time.

The eight ships of the fleet lay side by side and were a pretty sight with signal flags flying. It seemed as if all of Philadelphia had turned out to witness their departure. Ships and craft of all descriptions crowded the Delaware River, weighted to the gunnels with patriots and, it is safe to say, a goodly number of Tories. Bright colored pennants flipped and smacked, struck by icy draughts of wind blowing from the east. Ladies, well buried in garments and bonnets of wool, shook kerchiefs which frequently blew away from mittened hands.

The Philadelphia shore was jammed with people, as were the decks of the other naval ships. Only the *Alfred*'s deck had saved room for dignitaries and officers and their families, soon to arrive in all pomp and circumstance with Commodore Esek Hopkins.

It was January 14, 1776, just two days before Henry Lunt's twenty-third birthday—a bright, sunny day that sparkled on the river and flashed like diamonds from off the ice flo. It was nonetheless bitterly cold.

A cheer went up from the wharfside, and from the sudden commotion there, they surmised that the procession had arrived at the foot of Walnut Street.

Thomas Chase, assigned gunner on the lower deck, whispered in Lunt's ear, "Such weak huzzahs surely come from Tory throats." John Terry, his powder monkey, ever at his side, nodded agreement.

Henry Lunt frowned. He whispered back, "More likely is it that the Tory throats are stiffly silent."

The ceremonial barge had put off from the Philadelphia shore and was being both skulled and oared in their direction. Commodore Hopkins, postured like some inboard figurehead, stood rigidly apart from the others at the prow. Lunt thought he looked ridiculous. Huge ice cakes thumped at the sides of the barge causing the commodore to stagger. Henry Lunt wanted to laugh. However, he did not, but Thomas Chase did with an audible guffaw.

Lieutenant Jones frowned his displeasure, looking back over his shoulder at Henry Lunt who reddened, momentarily vexed at his friend, Thomas Chase. The latter, a long time acquaintance of Jones, held him not as much in awe as did the others. Lunt quickly cooled his anger. He owed much to Chase.

Since coming aboard the *Alfred*, Lunt had found much to stimulate his resentment by virtue of having been reduced in rank. Chase constantly placated him by pointing out the many factors to be learned, and also unlearned. He would caution, "Note the differences, Lunt. A ship of war is not a merchantman."

There were differences, but they could be learned. What was harder was the matter of personal pride. Captain Henry Lunt could not forget his rightful rank. He was proud of being a Lunt from Newbury, Massachusetts, a seafarer well schooled in his knowledge of the sea and sailing ships. A direct descendant of Henry Lunt, first settler of Newbury in the year 1630, he was prone to boast of this and point out that he was equal to any other.

By "any other," he meant Captain Dudley Saltonstall, in command of the *Alfred*. "His ancestor," Lunt would point out, was Sir Richard Saltonstall." "He came to our shores with others from Wiltshire in England and has since made much monies from his company formed for the raising of cattle, sheep, and horses—which we do have much need of."

On that day, Henry Lunt asked himself who should rightfully be the captain of the *Alfred*, he or Dudley Saltonstall.

There was no more time for dreaming or conjecture. The commodore's barge was at the side and he was being piped over by the bos'n. It was an emotional moment not to be denied.

There, on the *Alfred*'s deck, Henry Lunt stood at strict attention, his heart pounding as if to burst and tears forming in his eyes. Captain Dudley Saltonstall gave the signal, and John Paul Jones hoisted to the *Alfred*'s masthead the first flag ever to wave over an American naval ship. On that memorable occasion, it was not the Stars and Stripes but a banner fashioned of yellow silk, embossed with a rattlesnake and the motto, "Don't Tread on Me." The rattlesnake was cut into thirteen sections, one for each colony.

If Lieutenant Jones had had his way, American naval men would have been attired in a trim uniform similar to that of the Royal Navy. He would have selected red as the predominant color, not to imitate the foe as much as to lessen the horror of human blood, which gushed forth so freely to saturate the sands poured upon the gun decks.

Due to the impoverished condition of the Continental government, Jones was forced to accept the practical attire of the merchantman sailor. However, he saw to it that his people were frequently dipped in the ocean for cleanliness, and that they wore their long hair clubbed to the backs of their necks, ends stiff from a dip in the tar barrel.

John Paul Jones kept his gun deck well sanded, prepared at all times for battle. His guns were clean and ever ready. His gunners could be singled out from the others without effort because he kept their heads heavily covered—swathed in black to protect their ears and brains from the percussion of the cannon.

The pattern established by John Paul Jones was one of precision and timing. His gunners were practiced until their operation was second nature. They received hand signals from a gunner's mate who sang a little ditty that was hardly ever heard by his purposefully deafened gunners but was for him a metronome. The mate sang, "If I weren't a gunner, I wouldn't be here—forward, fire! If I weren't a gunner, I wouldn't be here—after, fire!"

The broadside was never fired all at once for the safety of the ship, which could be badly wracked from concussion. Guns from the top deck raked the rigging of the enemy, the ones below pounded the bowels.

Few men cared to cross Lieutenant Jones. The men under his command were chosen by him, and they knew it, because they accepted responsibility and discipline. They recognized a superior to the extent that they would obey his given orders at once and without question.

Jones had the ability to stimulate his men into the fun and games of war. There was, therefore, no resentment among them when they were still at duty while all other parts of the ship were at leisure.

Other operations aboard the *Alfred* were lax. The men were allowed to move about at will, loll on the decks, and play in the yards, vying with one another for first sight of an enemy sail. Denied to them was the lower gun deck, and many scoffed and poked fun at the peculiar lieutenant and his war games.

On the other hand, men under Jones seemed to enjoy and understand fully the fact that their superior had something better than idleness for them. Below on the second gun deck of the *Alfred*, they drilled and trained in preparation for war.

Jones described this in a letter to Joseph Hewes in which he wrote: "I formed an exercise and trained the men so well to the use of the great guns, they went through the motions of broadsides and rounds exactly as soldiers generally perform the manual exercise."

The Philadelphia Fleet, as it has commonly been called, moved first toward the Bahamas and made an unsuccessful attempt to capture Fort Nassau on one of the islands. Next of import came the historic and vainglorious running fight with the British sloop-of-war *Glasgow*. This took place off the east end of Long Island and was the first major engagement of the fleet.

It started on the fourth day of April when the Captain of the marines on the *Alfred* had just retired at midnight. The sails of the British ship were sighted. At half after one all hands were awakened and beaten to quarters. They were soon ready for action. The captain of the marines gave his account in a later investigation by, not the navy, but the Marine Committee. He told them:

> The main body of my company of Marines was placed on the main-deck. The remaining part, with my second lieutenant and myself, were placed on the quarter-deck. We soon discovered a large ship standing directly before us.
>
> The brigantine *Cabot* was foremost of the Fleet, the *Alfred* close after, not more than one hundred yards behind but to windward withal. When the *Cabot* came closer, she was hailed by the ship, which we then learned was the *Glasgow*, man-of-war.
>
> The brigantine immediately fired her broadside and instantly received a return of two-fold which, owing to the weight of metal, damaged her so much in her hull and rigging as to oblige her to retire for a while and refit.
>
> The *Alfred* then came in, not having it in our power before to fire without hurting our own ship. We engaged the *Glasgow* side by side for three glasses [a half hour] as hot as could be possible on both sides. The first broadside the *Glasgow* fired, my second lieutenant close by my side fell dead. He was shott by a musket ball from a British sharpshooter in the *Glasgow*'s tops and caught clean in the head. I might have been second but for the havoc of debris around me.
>
> Unfortunately for us, our main brace and tiller rope were shott away soon after the firing began, which caused our ship to broach too and gave the enemy an opportunity to rake us fore and aft. The battle continued until daylight, at which time the *Glasgow* made all sail she could crowd and stood in for Newport. At sunrise, the Commodore gave signal to give up the chase....

The attack on the *Glasgow* has been compared unfavorably to even the least of major sea battles. It might possibly have been erased from American history had it not been the first major and official attempt to distinguish itself by the Continental navy.

Commodore Esek Hopkins, although smarting with embarrassment under the wide-spread criticism he was receiving, sent his report to Congress in a communique dated at New London, Connecticut, on April 9, 1776, and received by that august body seven days later.

In that report, the commodore revealed that the *Alfred* had six men killed and many wounded. The *Cabot* had four men killed and seven wounded, including Captain John B. Hopkins, son of the commodore. One man on the *Columbus* lost his arm. The *Alfred* received great damage, the worst of which was having the wheel ropes and block shot away. This had given the *Glasgow* time to make sail.

Commodore Hopkins sent condolences to the kinfolk of Sinclair Seymour, master of the *Cabot*, and Lieutenant Fitzpatrick of the *Alfred*, both killed.

Members of the Congress read the reports with alarm. Incredible as it seemed, the truth was starkly simple: eight American war ships had been defeated by one British sloop-of-war.

## 9

## AFTER THE *GLASGOW*

The American fleet came limping into the harbor at New London, Connecticut, on April 15, 1776. All of the eight ships were in poor shape, as was revealed by the investigation which followed. The conclusion drawn was that the Americans had comported themselves like amateurs.

Commodore Hopkins, writing his report with embarrassment, was too proud to ask for sympathy even based on the fact that his own son had been wounded. He was subsequently dismissed, but he served, nevertheless, until December of 1776.

Hopkins had a fairness in his nature, and he called John Paul Jones before him to commend him for his performance in battle. Jones was flattered, but he knew that he had conducted his operation well, and he was taking no chances that this move to the fore might reverse the moment his back was turned. Smarting under public censure "of all seamen in the unfortunate *Glasgow* encounter," Jones wrote the following to Joseph Hewes protesting:

> The unfortunate engagement with the *Glasgow* seems to be a general reflection on the officers of the Fleet, but a little more reflection will set the matter right; for no officer under a superior who doth not stand charged by the superior for cowardice or misconduct can be blamed on any occasion whatever.
>
> For my part, I wish a general inquiry might be made respecting the abilities of the officers in all stations, and then this country would not be cheated. . . .

Jones expressed disappointment in the slack methods of

selecting officers and took the liberty of presenting his own qualifications, drawn from service in the British navy:

> I may be wrong, but in my opinion a commander in the Navy ought to be a man of strong and well-connected sense, with a tolerable education; a gentleman as well as a seaman, both in theory and practice. For, want of learning and rude ungentle manners are by no means characteristic of an officer.
>
> I have been led into this subject upon feeling myself hurt as an individual by the censures that have been indescriminately thrown out.
>
> I should esteem myself happy in being sent for to Philadelphia to act under the more immediate direction of the Congress, especially in one of the new ships. I must rely on your interest therein.

Jones was given command of the *Providence*, and he took with him from the *Alfred* Henry Lunt of Newbury, Massachusetts, Richard Dale of Virginia, and seven others. Several of these were later with Jones on the historic cruise of the *Bon Homme Richard*, but much was to happen ere that.

On May 10, 1776, a message was brought in by fast post riders. Originating from the floor of the second Continental Congress, the word was that General George Washington had been made Commander-in-Chief of the revolutionary forces, and he had been directed to raise an army of 20,000 men for defense. Esek Hopkins was ordered to give over 100 men from off the ships.

Lieutenant John Paul Jones on the *Providence* was assigned the duty to deliver these men to General Washington at New York. With his typical and rigid adherence to duty, Jones lost no time doing as he was bid. With the help of Richard Dale and Henry Lunt, they selected some of the best marksmen in the fleet. Jones then made one of the fast trips he was to become noted for and accomplished his entire assignment in thirty-six hours.

Some idea of the reigning confusion can be gathered from a letter written by Jones from New York to Joseph Hewes, when he reported: "I left the *Andrea Doria* and the *Cabot* at Rhode Island ready to sail together on a four-week cruise. What will become of the *Columbus* and the *Alfred,* heaven only knows."

(What actually happened to the *Alfred,* following repairs, ties in with later related events. That ship, in August of that same year, went on cruise with the *Raleigh,* a new frigate launched at Portsmouth, New Hampshire on May 21, 1776.)

Regarding the landing of the 100 men for General Washington at New York and subsequent plans for the *Providence,* Jones wrote: "I have landed the soldiers and will now apply myself to shipping men—if any are to be had."

Jones added, "It seems that the seamen almost to the man had entered the Army before the Fleet was set. I am well informed that there are four or five thousand seamen now in land service. When I have got what men are to be had here in New York, I am ordered back to Rhode Island for further instructions."

John Paul Jones worried constantly that he would somehow be superseded by those whose commissions came after his, and he was rightly apprehensive concerning this in the light of what subsequently happened. He wrote many letters to his friends in government in protest of the falsification and insecurity of his rank.

His irritation is expressed in the following letter to Hewes:

> There is little confidence to be placed in reports, otherwise the lieutenants of the fleet might have reason to be uneasy when they are told that the several committees have orders to appoint all officers for the new ships, excepting only the captains.
>
> I cannot think that they will be overlooked who have at the first stepped forth and shown at least a willingness. Nor can I suppose that my own conduct in service will, in the esteem of Congress, subject me to be superseded in favor of a younger officer, especially one who is said not to understand navigation—I mean the lieutenant of the *Cabot* who was put in command of the *Fly* at Reedy Island after I had declined it. This I did because I had been told no new commission would be given, and I considered the *Fly* a paltry message boat, fit to be commanded by a midshipman.
>
> I first declined command of the *Providence* at Phila-

delphia and would not now have accepted it if it had not been for the rude, unhappy temper of my late commander of the *Alfred*.

I now reflect with pleasure that I had a philosophy sufficient to avoid quarreling with him and that I had his blessing at parting. May he soon be of an even and affable disposition, and may he find pleasure in communicating happiness around him.

Upon my appointment to the *Providence* it was still without the rank of captain and I was indeed astonished to find my seniority questioned. The commodore told me he must refer to the Congress. I wish the matter in dispute might be cleared up.

I will cheerfully abide by whatever Mr. Hewes thinks is right. At the same time, I am ready at any time to have my pretensions inquired into by men who are judges.

When I applied for a lieutenancy, I hoped in that rank to gain much useful knowledge from men more experienced than myself. I was mistaken, however, for instead of gaining information I was obliged to inform others.

In the list of original appointments to the American navy, Jones was sixth from the top. He was somewhat mollified when he received his commission in this order on August 8, making him officially captain of the *Providence*.

But nothing seemed decided in those days, and when in the following October a resolution was passed in Congress declaring the order in which naval officers should take rank, Jones was placed eighteenth. He was filled with wrath when news of this reached him, but he was by this time completely involved with revolutionary war activity. That activity began on the *Providence*.

John Paul Jones was able to inspire men to incredible heights and incredible loyalties. Even so, the absence of money as reward for service was eventually to lose him many of his key men. Henry Lunt was one of these, but he did not leave until after the cruise of the *Providence*.

It was during the days at sea that Lunt was heard to boast of the Newburyport ships which could "outmaneuver and outrun any." The Newbury man's ranting certainly reached the captain's ears. Jones admitted to being jawed of the new naval ships by Henry Lunt until his ears were sore.

However, it is not clear just which ships Jones made reference to when he wrote to Joseph Hewes, "The largest and best of the frigates was launched the day after I left Providence, but from what I can learn neither of them [there must have been two] will equal the Philadelphia ships."

Jones probably did not allude to the ships being built at Portsmouth, New Hampshire, where the *America*, first on the ways, lay unfinished, while the *Raleigh*, the first frigate built there for the Continental government, was launched on May 21, 1776.

## 10

## VISIT TO SALISBURY POINT

Jones was under sealed orders from the Congress when he moved out of the Newport, Rhode Island, roadstead on June 13, 1776. When he was at sea, he opened his orders and found that his destination was one which would please Henry Lunt very much. The *Providence* was to proceed to Newburyport, Massachusetts, Lunt's home port—one of those chosen for the bringing in of prize ships.*

The order stated, "The ships of war are driven out of that bay, which is the safest to send in prizes of any on the continent." Additional instructions were that Jones was to capture and send to port for trial "any vessel thought to be acting detrimental to the interests of the American states." If this seemed permissiveness to the extreme—often resulting in the capture of ships of any and all countries—it was the same game that all were playing.

There were many prizes brought in at Newburyport and "much goods necessary to both existence and war" were delivered there. The sinking of the piers in the river proved to be a canny move after all, and the town of Newburyport gained prestige at the Continental Congress. It also advanced the status of Henry Lunt with Captain John Paul Jones, who probably really began to listen to Lunt in his boastful exploitation of Newburyport as a shipbuilding center.

The Newburyport townspeople were very much impressed at the sight of a native son walking together with the captain of the first American naval ship ever seen there. It's too bad that the

---

* See Appendix for visits to Newburyport.

visit was a short one. Nevertheless, Jones could have been well entertained at many fine homes and probably would have been—for he loved to be feted—had not the shipyards caught his shrewd and calculating eye. He discovered that Henry Lunt had not exaggerated the beauty of these very sturdy and fast sailing vessels.

A fortuitous note from Robert Morris, another member of the Marine Committee, caught up with the *Providence* at Newburyport and sent Jones on a quick trip up the river. With Henry Lunt as escort, he went by barge up the Merrimack to Salisbury Point where he met with thirty-one years old William Hackett, who had drawn up a new and altered design for ships-of-war that had been adopted by the Continental government. The first frigate in this new design, the *Raleigh*, had been completed in May at Portsmouth, New Hampshire, built under the supervision of William Hackett's brother, James.

Jones later reported to his friends on the Marine Committee that the Congress had not been remiss in its approval of the Hackett design. Secretly, he promised himself that he would command one of these ships, and he pompously announced to Henry Lunt that these same beautiful and fast ships would be just about perfect after he, Jones, had effected some changes.

Henry Lunt's visit to Newburyport was not the happy one he had hoped it would be. John Paul Jones kept him so busy he spent little time at home, and this made his wife Sarah very much out of sorts. When he did see his family, they were full of woe. Only his father, Matthew Lunt, the one bearing the brunt of it all, did not complain. This patriot-farmer was adamant in his insistence that he would manage with the help of the women while his sons made war. Staying at the Newbury farm house were Ezra's wife and family and Henry's wife and four-month-old son, a rosy-cheeked, blonde bouncer.

Ezra, who had re-enlisted in the Continental army, was in command of a company serving under Colonel Moses Little at Long Island. Word filtering back home pessimistically proclaimed that the colonial forces at their location were being pushed back.

Even more disturbing was the condition of Henry's second eldest brother, Daniel, who was making slow recovery from a grueling experience as a prisoner at sea of the British.

Henry Lunt was also financially embarrassed. Caught in an enlistment he enjoyed, but which had netted him no pay so far, he had run out of money with which to support his family. He found himself lending a more than casual interest to whispered plans for a privateering venture, already entered into by several of his kinfolk. Lunt was being pressured at a time when he was most vulnerable. There can be no doubt that Daniel's experience gave him the final push.

Earlier in the year 1776, at the same time that Henry Lunt was setting forth with the Philadelphia Fleet, Captain Daniel Lunt was sailing with his merchant ship into danger.* On February 17, while on a homeward passage from Grande Tierre at about two leagues distance from Cape Ann at Gloucester, Massachusetts, his ship fell in with and was taken by the British sloop-of-war *Lively*, sailing under the command of a Captain Bishop. The captives and their brig were taken into Boston Harbor and put aboard the *Renown*, a prison ship commanded by a Captain Banks. The treatment received by the Americans is described by Captain Daniel Lunt in a communication later written by him to the Newburyport Committee of Safety and Correspondence. In this, he provides a firsthand description of one such incident. (Significant of the town's reluctance to enter into a war is the fact that the captain's letter was not entered into the town records until April 19, the day of the Lexington and Concord incidents.)

The letter states:

> As we came on board the *Renown*, Captain Banks ordered us, with bundles of clothing, bedding and so forth, to the quarter deck. He then called for the second lieutenant and master-at-arms to search our beds and to overhaul all of our bundles of clothes to see if there was money amongst them. Then, turning to us, he said, "I will search you myself, and that well, too, you scoundrels."
> Whilst they were opening and searching our bundles, they

---

* See Bibliography, item 5.

began stripping off our clothes, quickly searching every place in the linings where even a farthing might be concealed. And they continued the whole time breathing all sorts of induff upon us for no crime, or supposed crime, other than having been born an American.

After getting us through this new and unnatural procedure, robbing me of four johannes and Captain Ephraim Little of 100 more, he called for and delivered us up to the boatswain. He was ordered to take us to the main deck where we were kept in constant hard labor and, if we declined or faltered, were soundly flogged.

We, and by this I mean even all of the masters of American vessels, were kept at the most ignominious tasks on board and were loaded with curses and reproaches from the principal officers even after we readily complied with their unrighteous and inhuman commands.

We learned that our punishment was because we had not been found up in arms against our own country. We were constantly commanded and insulted without right to reply by men far inferior to those formerly under our commands, having the breath of hell constantly inflaming our ears informing us that our torments would be perpetual and that we would never again set foot upon American ground.

Thus did these devices of torment ultimately intimidate some Americans, weakened as they were by short rations and inadequate clothing against the winter cold. They therefore judged themselves excusable and yielded to British solicitation and entered in service aboard their ships. We who refused intimidation were sent on board an East Indiaman with the assurance that we were going to be sent to those islands, there to be kept in slavery at hard labor for the rest of our lives.

Worn out with continued fatigue and constant reproaches, half frozen because my clothing had been stolen from me, I grew sick of life. I resolved at all hazards to attempt an escape or die trying. In the night between the twentieth and twenty-first of March, last, I managed to cut away a boat from alongside and, with others, got ashore on Point Shirley.

I publish this narrative, upon being influenced, not only in the name of truth but due to the earnest desire of a number of American ship masters who still labor under these distressing circumstances.

Whilst I made agreement with my brethren in bondage that I would, if successfully escaped, proceed at once to acquaint General Washington with their plight, I have been so poor in health I could not go.

Daniel Lunt's communication so shook the members of the Committee of Correspondence and Public Safety at Newburyport that they voted: "That the printers on the continent be hereby desired to publish the narrative of Captain Daniel Lunt, and we do hereby certify that the said Captain Lunt was born and brought up among us and is esteemed a man of truth, and we think full credit may be paid to said narrative."

## 11

## VOYAGE OF THE *PROVIDENCE*

Things were going quite well from the viewpoint of John Paul Jones. The trip to Newburyport had proved to be quite exciting, and he could hardly wait to make his report on the new design for warships by William Hackett of Salisbury Point. He was especially attentive to Henry Lunt at this time, but he had no interest in Lunt's personal problems.

Captain Jones would have been interested to the point of vexation had he known what his second lieutenant (this was Lunt's unofficial title conferred by Jones) had been up to. Had Jones not been diverted by other things, he might have learned that Lunt had signed up to go privateering as soon as his present enlistment expired—advance pay was already in his father's hands. In the meantime, there was a cruise to be undertaken.

They put the *Providence* to sea after five days at Newburyport and thereby missed an order from Esek Hopkins to sail to Boston.\* They took a few minor prizes in merchant ships and sent them into Newburyport Harbor before orders caught up with them which again changed their position on the Atlantic Ocean.

Jones soon discovered that he had a prime complement of men on the *Providence*, most of them northeast Yankees, and he was elated with their seamanship. In supreme confidence, he moved them out of Delaware on August 21 under his new orders, which allowed him more freedom than before in his pursuit of prizes. He was remarkably successful. By early September, the *Providence* had taken three prizes. It had also had a very narrow escape from an English frigate after a chase of six hours, part of the time within pistol shot. This harrowing experience sent Jones

---

\* See Appendix B, p. 210

into one of his characteristic periods of physical exhaustion. He stood his vessel in at a safe haven where he alternately rested and proliferated into a storm of letter writing. During this time, Richard Dale kept house, and Henry Lunt kept the crew in shape.

While his ship was being cleaned and mended, Jones wrote, among others, a letter to the Marine Committee at Philadelphia giving an account of his ship's activities, including their escape from the English frigate:

> I had the honor on the 27th of August writing the Committee per the brigantine *Britania*, sent under the care of Lieutenant William Grinnell as a prize.
>
> On the first current, we fell in with a fleet of five sail, one of a British frigate of twenty-six guns upon one deck alone. She sailed fast and pursued us by the wind till after four hours chase, unluckily for us, the sea turned very cross and she got within musket shott of our lie quarter. As they had continued firing upon us from the first without showing colors, I now ordered ours to be hoisted and began firing at them. Upon this, they also hoisted American colors, and they fired guns to the leeward. But, the bait would not take. For, having everything prepared I bore away before the wind and set all our light sail at once, so that before her sails could be trimmed and steering sails set, we were almost out of reach of cannon shott.
>
> Our hairbreadth escape and saucy manner of making it must have mortified them not a little. Had they foreseen this motion and been prepared to counteract it, they might have fired several broadsides of double-headed and grape shott, which would have done us very material damage. But they were bad marksmen, and though we were within pistol range, not one did touch the *Providence* of the many they did fire.
>
> Last night, we took the Bermuda-built brigantine, *Sea Nymph*, bound from Barbadoes to London with a cargo of rum, sugar, ginger, oil, pipes and best Madiera wine. The brig is new and sails fast so that she is a pretty good prize. By the master of the brig, I hear that the *Andrea Doria* was off Bermuda a few days since.

The successful cruise of the *Providence* provided stimulus for Henry Lunt and relieved his character of stigma over the rediculous *Glasgow* encounter, which had been aired about. Under the invincible Captain Jones, he, along with many others of the *Providence*, began to believe in his own indestructibility.

When on October 17, 1776, Jones, in a customary procedure, summoned his people to stand amid ship to learn the summation of their productive cruise, this is the report that they heard:

Prizes manned and sent in:
  Brigantine *Britania*, whaler
  Brigantine *Sea Nymph*, West Indiaman
  Brigantine *Favourite*, West Indiaman
  Brigantine *Success*, Jersey, Newfoundland
  Brigantine *Kingston Packet*, Jamaica
  Brigantine *Defiance*, Jersey, Newfoundland
  Ship *Alexander*, Jersey, Newfoundland
  Sloop *Portland*, whaler

Prizes burnt or destroyed:
  Ship *Adventure*, Jersey, Newfoundland
  Brig *Friendship*, Jersey, Newfoundland
  Schooner *John*, London
  Schooner *Betsy*, Jersey
  Schooner *Betsy*, Halifax
  Schooner *Sea Flower*, Canso
  Schooner *Ebenezer*, Canso
  Schooner *Hope*, Canso

With the counting of their united gains, each man on the *Providence* was also counting his personal gains, but he was building castles in air. Midway in September, Joseph Hewes sent word to Jones that a wage scale had now been set by the Congress. Jones knew the men would balk at it. Able seamen were to receive eight dollars, ordinary seamen six dollars, and landsmen two-thirds of a dollar per month. The scale was poor enough, but the unacceptable aspect was that all prizes were to be the property of the American states, with no mention of if or when each man might receive a share—something each had been led to believe he might expect when he enlisted.

Jones badly wanted to hold his able seamen of the *Providence* to his side. He now knew that he was soon to be in command of the *Alfred*, cleaned and ready once more for sea duty.

Some of the *Providence* complement would go with Jones, but not Henry Lunt. That member of the crew was tired of being on a par with the able seaman. He desperately needed money, which he knew how to get, and, anyway, he was committed to try his hand at privateering.

In desperation, Jones, who knew now and too late what was happening all about him, wrote to Commodore Hopkins urging that the men be sent a share of prize money at once. The commodore contacted the Marine Committee, stating: "It will be very difficult to man any ships further without prize money for the crew as good as on privateers, which is one-half, and large sums advanced before they go to sea."

There seems to have been a degree of success here. By October 24, changes had taken place which placed Jones on the *Alfred* in command of a cruise which would outdo his performance on the *Providence* and secure his status with the Marine Committee.

His look-alike, Henry Lunt, took a different course; one which was to identify him with a government-commissioned privateer, a marauder of the sea no more than the official naval ship, but of doubtful status in the eyes of many. When he might have covered his name with reflected glory under Captain Jones, Lunt elected instead the inglorious route of capture by the British and two years in prison. Still, destiny works its ends, and it took a hand when Lunt, after much travail, was reunited with Jones by means of a cartel exchange of prisoners on the other side of the Atlantic Ocean. Lunt was thus with Commodore Jones on the historic cruise of a fleet led by the *Bon Homme Richard*.

After his service with Jones on the *Providence*, Lunt returned to Newburyport where his patriotic ire was further aroused by news from the battle front. Brother Ezra was still with General George Washington's forces the last Henry knew, under retreat when Sir William Howe and his British army won the battle of Long Island. Additional bad news revealed that the Americans had suffered another put-down at White Plains, where Ezra had suffered a slight wound. The wound was enough to bring him home for a temporary stay, and there he found Henry and Daniel waiting for the privateer *Dalton* to put to sea.

The brothers had a fine reunion, one of the last they were to enjoy together for five long years. Ezra was the first to leave. Moving cautiously where intelligence led him, he was to rejoin Washington's retreating army around November 28, somewhere in Pennsylvania, opposite New Jersey and just over the Delaware River.

The men by name of Lunt were moving toward a notable coincidence. For Daniel, Henry, Richard, and Cutting Lunt, the night of December 26, 1776 would spell defeat and capture by the British. For Ezra Lunt it would be one of triumph in the turning of the tables by General Washington, for Ezra would be there to aid in the capture of one thousand Hessians at Trenton, New Jersey after he had followed Washington across the Delaware on Christmas night.

John Paul Jones, it must be added, neither understood nor sympathized with the reasons given by Henry Lunt for leaving naval service for privateering. Jones wrote to Robert Morris prior to his cruise:

> I found the *Alfred* with only thirty men. We have, with much ado, enlisted thirty more, but it seems the privateers entice them away. The common class of mankind are actuated by no nobler purpose and principle than that of self-interest. This, and this only, determines all adventurers in privateers, the owners as well as those they employ.
>
> Without a respecktable Navy, alas, America!

## 12

## THE PRIVATEER *DALTON*

Revolutionaries were divided in their opinions concerning privateering, even after the Continental Congress, on April 3, 1776, adopted a series of resolutions giving private ships-of-war letters of marque and reprisal. The Congress, at once, sent out blank commissions to governors and councils of their several colonies to be delivered to persons "within the right to receive them."

It was several weeks after that before the governor of Massachusetts and others issued commissions to ship owners. But once the plan was set in motion, commissions were delivered wholesale. No town sent in more, nor received more, than did Newburyport, the richest mercantile center in the North.

The records do not reveal any large success for the privateers which, letters of marque notwithstanding, were no match for Britain's mighty navy. Prisoners were taken, placing hundreds of American seaman, badly needed to man the new American ships, either at the bottom of the ocean or in British prisons on both sides of the water.

All of this was an accomplished fact when William Whipple of Portsmouth, on July 2, 1778, confided to Josiah Bartlett of Amesbury his opinion on the matter.* Whipple wrote, "Had there been no privateers, possibly we might have had a larger number of publick ships."

Whipple gave two reasons for this strongly expressed opinion. "First, no kind of business can so effectually introduce luxury, extravagance and every kind of dissipation that tend to the

---

* See Bibliography, item 14.

destruction of morals of people. Second, men on privateers tend to lose their concepts of right and wrong, and they develop insatiable avarice with the property of enemies of their country and they will, without compunction, seize even friends."

Whipple concluded his argument with a melancholy commentary on the ambivalance of viewpoint, saying, "But, then, what incentive is there for men to join the Navy when even they are treated with contempt—which a man of any feeling at all cannot bear."

The privateer *Dalton* was a microcosm illustrating the essential failure within the practice of privateering and was probably the most ambitious effort attempted at Newburyport. The ship was prepared during the summer and autumn of 1776, and despite a complement of 120 of the most able seamen of the area* she was no match for a British man-of-war. The ship, a brigantine, was named for her chief sponsor, Tristram Dalton, and her first voyage was her last. Yet, the *Dalton* is the privateer most mentioned of all of those to sail out of Newburyport, and one reason for this is that two members of her crew kept very accurate diaries.** Another reason is that the *Dalton's* complement included many who had been in service to the Continental navy, some even under John Paul Jones, including, of course, Henry Lunt.

On October 7, 1776, after having been clumsily converted from a merchantman to a ship-of-war, the *Dalton* was commissioned a privateer. Eleazer Johnson of Newburyport, the captain, signed the petition on her behalf and on behalf of her sponsors, Tristram Dalton and Stephen Hooper. The petition also asked that Daniel Lunt be commissioned as master of the *Dalton*. Ordered in Governor's Council of Massachusetts on October 10, Lunt's commission was added. The Lunt family was well represented. Ezra and Paul were soldiers of the army, but Richard and Cutting Lunt, brothers of Paul, and Henry Lunt, brother of Daniel, were all there. Officers of the *Dalton* were chosen for their position in the community of Newburyport and for seniority in age and not in knowledge of warfare. Therefore, in spite of

* See Appendix C, p. 214.
** See Bibliography, items 2 and 3.

their numbers, only Daniel of the Lunt family received a commission.

Once again, Henry was to feel the sting of neglect, but his loyalty to family, and his dedication to the cause, were now stronger than any thoughts of self-advancement.

The *Dalton* mounted eighteen carriage guns and sixteen swivels, and Henry Lunt, looking about in dismay, realized that her decks were overcrowded. But he found nobody, not even his brother, Daniel, who would listen to his reasonable arguments for a few changes and a lightening of the load. The *Dalton*, it seemed, carried a gallant but naive complement when it came to games of war at sea.

The *Dalton* was taken by the British in short order. After taking on officers and crew from the Newburyport area, she was put to sea on November 15, 1776, and sailed northward up the coast. The following day she was put in at Portsmouth and hidden out in Pepperill's Cove in Portsmouth Harbor. She immediately came alive with activity. For seven days she took on crew in groups of four and five so as not to attract attention. As the men came over the side, they were taken before the master for assignment and instruction. As Daniel Lunt fulfilled his obligations, Henry stood ever ready at his elbow to assist whenever he was needed.

It took two more days after the boarding of her full complement to ready the privateer for sea, and on the ninth day, they again sailed forth, this time with grim purpose. It was almost a lark at first. Between November 28 and December 23, the *Dalton* chased a sloop she could not catch, likewise a French brig and a Danish snow. Her luck was to change for the worse.

On the day before Christmas, the American privateer fell in with one of the largest of the British ships-of-war in the area. It was the *Reasonable* of sixty-four guns. This great ship was sighted by the lookout at two o'clock in the afternoon. To close with this ship was unthinkable, thus they had to try to outdistance her.

For the next six hours, the Yankee merchant sailors performed every known maneuver to break away, but against such overwhelming odds their efforts were in vain. Like doom, the *Reasonable* drew ever closer and finally closed in. It was now eleven o'clock at night, and they were in latitude 44, north longitude ¼ west, with a light breeze blowing.

The *Reasonable* opened fire! The situation was preposterous. The *Dalton*, without firing a shot, surrendered.

Henry Lunt, of all, was most mortified. Here was the *Glasgow* put-down all over again. Inwardly he cursed the fate that had placed him on the *Dalton* instead of with the invincible John Paul Jones. Outwardly, he agreed that even Jones would have surrendered against such insurmountable odds. It was bad luck, that was all.

Now it was survival at stake, and Daniel Lunt, for one, openly wept that he was once more taken a prisoner. British marines with drawn swords poured onto the *Dalton*'s deck and then put their swords away at the sight of the colonial bumkins drawn stiffly to attention in their makeshift uniforms. Formalities were rudely abandoned as the American privateersmen were jostled, knocked to the deck, and otherwise roughly treated in the process of herding them over to the *Reasonable*. Scorning such a makeshift prize, they stripped the *Dalton*, opened her sea cocks, and sent her to the bottom.

Prepared for the worst, the Americans came near to receiving it. They were crammed like cattle in the hold of the *Reasonable* and kept there during a long journey to England. Once a day, they were permitted to come above, and, much as they had to have the new air in their lungs, they dreaded it. They were constant prey to British sailors who vandalized them or struck them down when the whim suited. The voyage seemed so endless that even death at the end of a yardarm seemed preferable.

At Plymouth Harbor in England, they were transferred en mass to the prison ship *Belleisle* where conditions proved no better. After eighteen more days, they were removed to the *Torbay*, a man-of-war of seventy-four guns. It was under the command of a Captain St. John who provided them agonies in earnest. Samuel Cutler, one diary keeper on the *Dalton*, wrote, "The people are removed from cable tier to the twixt decks where there is a pen so small that all cannot lie down at one time." By the time the next removal came in six days, on February 13, 1777, many of the Americans were ill from privation and exposure. Then they ran into a piece of luck.

Captain George Broyer of the warship *Buford* was both kind and humane. When it was called to his attention that some of the Americans were ill, he ordered them sent at once to the royal hospital on land. Fortunate enough to go were Thomas and Nathaniel Bayley, Daniel Cottle, Ebenezer Hunt, Rueben Tucker, and Jonathan Whitmore, all of Newburyport; Joseph Clark of Boston, Daniel Lane of New Gloucester, and Will Horner of Ireland. Cottle and Hunt died, Lane later escaped, and Clark, Horner and Whitmore, yielded, at last, to pressure being put upon them all to join the British navy.

The Americans realized that much of the treatment they had received was to force them into service with the enemy. This had the opposite effect with most, whose hatred of the British increased with each passing day, and all anyone wished was to somehow gain freedom to go home.

Homesickness was the worst sickness of all, and rebellion was the worst part of strategy. Men of the Lunt family had a talent for survival, and they were more shrewd than some in their actions. They soon discovered that by volunteering for heavy duty, they could keep themselves above the cramped quarters below and could breathe in the fresh sea air. Such activity served also to keep their muscles fit and to serve them opportunities to keep a sharp watch on activities in Plymouth Harbor. Who knew when the opportunity to try for an escape might come?

They marked the comings and goings of many ships, including the last sailing to America of the *Somerset* of seventy-four guns. This was the same *Somerset* which figured in the opening battles at Lexington and Concord, and the same ship which later foundered off the New England coast, never to see England again. By that foundering, the *Somerset* figured as an instrument in providing crewmen for the sailing of a new American frigate, the *Alliance*, later that same year.

Eighty British sailors from off the *Somerset*, rescued from the sea by Americans, were on board the *Alliance* on her maiden voyage to France. They had volunteered their services so that they might be exchanged for American prisoners once they were back on their own side of the water.

The same Americans who would be exchanged for them had watched the *Somerset*'s departure from Plymouth Harbor without a premonition of events to come. How could they know that the *Alliance* was even then in the building, or that some of them would eventually be aboard her with John Paul Jones, fighting once again for an independent America?

## 13

## OLD MILL PRISON

From the end of March to the first of April, there was much sickness aboard the *Buford* with the *Dalton* people having their share. Near the second week in May, Joseph Hatch of Boston and Samuel Skriggins of Kittery died. That same day came the fourth move: to the *Blenheim* of ninety guns and Captain Hartwell.

June was the month in which the trials for high treason were held, and all were found guilty, as expected. Sentences were uniformly pronounced, sending officers as well as men to Old Mill Prison at Plymouth for an indefinite period, which could mean the rest of their lives. Then began the really bad times that drove several of the *Dalton's* people to defect to the British, and undermined the health of many more.

By June 22, 1777, all were physically in rough shape—badly clothed and poorly fed. The prisoners met up with many other Americans as desperate as they, from off other privateers captured by the British. Escape attempts were frequent, but few succeeded in getting away. When any did escape, retaliation against those remaining was swift and cruel.

A clear example of this was demonstrated on July 4, when John Knowlton of Newburyport, cashier of the *Dalton*, and Phineas Smith, master of the *Charming Sally*, ran away from the royal hospital. Immediately, Henry Lunt, Francis Little of Newburyport, and Dr. Samuel Smith of Hampton, New Hampshire, all from off the *Dalton*, were sent to the "itchy prison."

The itchy prison was a dark, vermin ridden hole in the ground and was, as its title implied, purposely infested. Those incarcerated there "went fair out of their minds," being plagued day and night until they found a half cure. By mixing dirt from "Hell's own floor" with some of their meagre water rations, they made a mud plaster with which they coated their flesh.

Also punished at that time was John George of Newburyport, who with others was placed in the "black hole," a nearby dungeon kept in total blackness. As they became accustomed to the dim light of their surroundings in the itchy prison, and conquered their discomfiture, at least in part, Henry Lunt and his companions began to look about for possible means of escape—an activity never out of their minds. They discovered that they were in a huge, stone-walled cistern with drains running off it. These drains, while damp, were no longer in use and were high enough for a man to walk through upright, although few tried it.

Henry Lunt did try it, and he soon discovered a drain leading directly to the black hole, which was simply another huge cistern. Lunt busied himself at once plotting an escape. On the morning of July 12, between the hours of three and four, Lunt, Little, Dr. Smith, and George, plus two others from the black hole, made their way through the "drain of the vault" and reached the free air outside the prison. Only the doctor made good his escape.

One at a time, in heartbreaking sequence, they were apprehended at varying places and brought back to Mill Prison. Henry Lunt and two others were last to be returned, under the armed guard of soldiers. They had somehow traveled all the way to Falmouth, thirty miles away. It seems sure that the Americans had a share of friends among the British who helped spirit them along by means of a well organized underground. There also were a goodly share of Britishers who were not friendly and lost no time in turning them in.

A description of Old Mill Prison will reveal that it was not easy to crack. The prison was a massive, stone structure in the center of an extensive court surrounded by a high stone wall. Twenty feet beyond the first wall was a second wall parallel to the first and completely surrounding it. The only openings in either wall were the gates. The inner gate was the stronger with huge iron bars eight feet high.

The outer gate was left open during the day for the convenience of the sentinels whose homes were just outside, and the prisoners were never allowed in the outer court. They were permitted to move about in the inner court from eight o'clock in the morning to sunset, after which they were locked in the gray, vermin infested prison.

Sentinels were stationed at the gates, on the walls, and among the prisoners. In spite of this constant surveillance, the Americans were hard to hold, and they never gave up no matter what the punishment.

The prisoners united in an ambitious project on July 18, 1777, that would spell freedom for some and further hardship for others. They began to dig a passage sixteen feet underground beneath the wall to an adjacent field. Somehow, they succeeded, and on Tuesday, August 5, the mass exodus was on. At eleven o'clock at night, when the sentinels relaxed in the belief nothing could happen, men began to go through the passage. It being small, several large people unfortunately "worried" the dirt down and narrowed the passage. It became a tight squeeze.

As it was, thirty-two men got out undiscovered before daylight, and seventeen of them were *Dalton* men, including Captain Eleazer Johnson, Master Daniel Lunt, and Lieutenants. Anthony Knapp and John Buntin. Nearly half of those who escaped, including Buntin, were brought back over a period of time. Lunt and Johnson made good their escape and thereby missed an opportunity to serve with John Paul Jones.

Disease plagued the prisoners, smallpox the most serious. Those who did not die were badly disfigured. Samuel Lambert of Martha's Vineyard, off the sloop *Charming Sally*, had a "horrible loss of the sight of his right eye when a pustule burst in it."

The prisoners were often deprived of food or stinted to the point of malnutrition. Henry Lunt, William Smith, and Josiah George, who were on half allowance or one ounce of beef, one quarter pound of bread, and a half pint of small beer per man for a twenty-four hour period, found something to lift their spirits when they were brought word that Captain John Lee of Newbury and his privateer brig *Fancy* had been taken by the British man-of-war *Fordroyant*. Captain Lee had news of home.

It was cheering news for Henry Lunt as he learned that his loved ones were well. On the other hand, he grieved for them that they knew nothing of his predicament and thought that all hands on the *Dalton* had probably been sunk at sea. Well, soon they would know better, or at least he hoped so, when Captain

Johnson and brother Daniel arrived back in Newburyport.

Captain Lee also brought news of the war. General Washington had recrossed the Delaware and, after his victory at Trenton, defeated the British at Princeton. Lunt was certain and rightly, that brother Ezra had participated in that victory, and it was all he could do to contain the enthusiasm he would have imprudently expressed.

After Daniel's escape, Henry Lunt took comfort in the companionship of Richard and Cutting Lunt, who seemed to have a far better knack for staying out of trouble than their cousin, Henry. Whenever circumstances of prison life allowed, the three engaged in long reminiscences of old times—when life was a series of the homecomings and departures that enlivened the life of a sailor. All longed for the good old days when a quick run to the Indies on a merchant ship paid a man well.

Henry thought of the days on the *Providence* and, in retrospect, fancied himself once more in the role of the deep sea marauder. The regret he now felt for not having remained under the command of the seemingly indestructible John Paul Jones was reflected in the glowing accounts he gave of the cruise of the *Providence*, and he never failed to excite envy with his true, but sometimes exaggerated, stories.

Sessions with Richard and Cutting were followed by periods of melancholia. News sifted in from time to time as other Americans were brought in, and it is almost certain that much of the dialogue centered around the new ships being built at Portsmouth, New Hampshire and Salisbury Point, Massachusetts. It is highly possible, even, that they knew John Paul Jones to be in command of one of those ships. If so, the news must have added to Henry Lunt's frustrations. It could have accounted for his repeated efforts to break out of prison long after many had desisted and resigned themselves to wait. Meanwhile, he built the man Jones larger and larger until his name became a rallying point for the other prisoners as well.

Tension was building up among the Americans caught in the Old Mill Prison, and, without their ever knowing, events and Henry Lunt were priming them for service with John Paul Jones. This was bourne out when, by cartel exchange, they were given their freedom, only to sign up almost to the man for service in the American navy.

By September 1777, the defiant Americans were being punished with so much frequency and were so gaining in numbers, it became necessary to build another black hole to accommodate the rebellious. At that time, Gideon Warren of Berwick died of putrid fever and smallpox. William Smith of Ireland and Henry Lunt, who was constantly being punished, were allowed to return to the upper prison from the black hole after being there for forty days. That was enough for Smith, and he signed up with the British. Twenty-two other persons on half allowance were returned to the upper prison to make room for sixteen more in the itchy prison.

In protest of the harsh treatment they were receiving, the Americans filed a writ with a Commissioner Bell. The keeper and turnkeys immediately filed their own protest, claiming that they had never worked harder in their lives nor suffered more insubordination. As might be expected, the prisoners got the worst of it. Mr. Bell ordered the one pence allowance to each American prisoner "by some kind gentleman" stopped at once. This was one example of some such acts of kindness attempted by the English people living in the vicinity of Old Mill prison.

While the sailors of the ill-fated *Dalton* were mourned as dead by their families and friends back home, new things were happening in America. The government of France was providing strong support for America, and although the prisoners at Old Mill in Plymouth, England knew little of it, America was striving for a navy while Benjamin Franklin and John Paul Jones were among those working for their release by cartel exchange.

For the sake of tying events together, it is now necessary to look in on Jones and his activities, as well as on other happenings designed to bring them all together again.

*Part Two*

## 14

## THE *RANGER*

When Henry Lunt journeyed to Philadelphia in the winter of 1775 to join the American navy, he did so with the full knowledge that ships-of-war were to be built in his own neighborhood. Like John Paul Jones, he wanted to be among the first on hand when commissions were being handed out, and he was more than disappointed when his hopes were dashed at the very onset.

Five months later, after the *Glasgow*, when Lunt had learned to respect and trust Jones and had yielded to what he recognized as a superior knowledge over his own, he told the captain about the New England ships.

The fact of the matter was that Jones already knew of the new ships, but in his canny way he withheld his knowledge. He chose instead to use this device in a manner of praise for his look-alike, and he expressed surprise and complete pleasure in Lunt's confidence. Thus did he wheedle the Newburyport man into taking him to Salisbury Point to see the Hackett design at first hand and to talk with William Hackett himself. But Jones would have to wait a bit longer—until after his command of the *Alfred*—before he finally was given command of one of the new ships.

The Revolutionary War was not going well for the Americans. American privateers were running into ill luck all of the time, and American seamen were pouring into British prisons at an alarming rate.

Admiral Graves of the British-American fleet was very self-satisfied, most of the time at anchor in Boston Harbor. He toasted his boots at many a Tory hearth while boasting of an early and permanent victory.

Meanwhile, down in Philadelphia, exhilarated by its fleet of eight ships, Congress was making further plans. On December 13, 1775, it was decided to enlarge the American navy with some new ships. Members of the Marine Committee were listening to three of their members, all of whom hailed from New England, the shipbuilding center. These gentlemen were John Langdon of Portsmouth, Josiah Bartlett of Amesbury, and William Whipple.

Bartlett had the shipbuilders! Before he left for Philadelphia and the decisive meeting with Congress, he stopped at the home of William Hackett of Salisbury Point to alert this designer and master shipbuilder that the time had come for the culmination of their long months of planning. William, it was agreed, would go with Bartlett to Philadelphia, while his brother, James, also a master builder, remained at home to gather materials for the building program they now knew was certain to get underway.

If Josiah Bartlett had the builders, John Langdon had the ideal location for building ships in secret. This was Langdon's Island in Portsmouth Harbor. A conflict between Bartlett and Langdon was avoided (for Langdon also had master builders) when a compromise was accepted by both. As a result, it was decided that William Hackett would remain at Salisbury Point to make use of the materials already on hand and to "keep to his designs." Early in 1776, his brother, James, was ordered to proceed to Portsmouth to help build ships for the government.*

When James arrived in Portsmouth, he was introduced to Captain Benjamin Remick, and the two proceeded to hit it off at once. As a result they worked in harmony side by side and built ships that were the models used by later, better-remembered builders—ships based on the designs of William Hackett that were used for American naval ships far into the future.

James Hackett found Langdon's Island to his liking. It was large and dark with pine so tall that masts of ships could be stepped without being sighted from the shore. But, no foe could get near the shore due to garrison batteries set up on either side.

There were other craftsmen at Portsmouth with full knowledge and skill in the building of ships. One was Paul Thomas Thompson, a favorite of Langdon but a thorn in the side of James Hackett, who regarded Thompson's ideas as radical and unsettled, always in constant change.

* See Bibliography, Item 9.

The first ship on the ways was the *America*, a huge frigate which could not possibly be manned at that time, so it was temporarily abandoned, not to be finished until six years later.

The *Raleigh*, therefore, was the first frigate to be built. Of 697 tons burden, her keel was laid on Langdon's Island on March 21, 1776, and she was completed just sixty days later. She was outfitted and launched on May 21. As might have been expected, there was a choosing of sides during the *Raleigh*'s building, with Paul Thomas Thompson influential in his home bailiwick and coming out ahead. He was, therefore, named master builder over James Hackett in a reversal of roles just when the *Raleigh* was nearly finished.

Hackett, who felt that Thompson, a ship captain, was probably far better at that than at shipbuilding, was ready to call it quits and go home. He was dissuaded, however, when Langdon, in a diplomatic coup, accomplished two things. He had Thompson named captain of the *Raleigh* and he reinstated Hackett as master builder, thereby placating both factions.

In August, the *Raleigh* joined up with the *Alfred* and sailed for France, where military stores obtained through the efforts of Benjamin Franklin were waiting for transportation to America.

James Hackett, the master builder now free of Thompson's harrassment, began work at once laying the keel of the famous sloop-of-war *Ranger* of 308 tons burden. Here was the new ship which would be given to the command of Captain John Paul Jones who, before the *Ranger* was half ready, would arrive in Portsmouth to harrass James Hackett as much as Thompson had ever done.

The day that John Paul Jones would remember as one of pride and major fulfillment was June 14, 1777, when he was commissioned by Congress as Captain of the *Ranger*, one of the new ships he had so long coveted.

In a second act on that same day, Congress designated the Stars and Stripes as the official flag of the new nation. This dual action was regarded by Jones as having great significance, and he came to look upon the American flag and John Paul Jones as synonymous. Seriously sentimental, his spirit flew with the colors from every masthead of the new navy. He believed that the Congress had recognized the ardor of his commitment to his adopted country. From that time on, with reverence toward the

American emblem ever in his heart, he was to fight fiercely and honestly for American independence.

The chairman of the Marine Committee wrote to Jones on June 18, 1777, ordering that he proceed at once to Portsmouth, where he was to "use diligence in outfitting the *Ranger.*" If there was one thing Jones was not noted for it was diligence—at least not when this was in conflict with perfection. Due to Jones's insistence upon certain specifications, the sloop-of-war was not ready until early October.

After his arrival in Portsmouth, Captain Jones lost no time in getting out to Langdon's Island, a beehive of activity. Not waiting for a formal introduction, he swept like a whirlwind over the *Ranger,* immediately full of complaints. Fault-finding at once, he paved the way for the changes he knew he would eventually demand, but he was actually more pleased with what he found than he was ready to admit.

Jones boarded at the Purcell-Lord house, and while he was lionized by the wealthy and influential, especially the ladies, he kept an eagle eye on his ship. He managed to remain aloof from entanglements, while the friendships he made proved lasting. One of these was with the family of John Wendell, a prominent Portsmouth patriot.

John Wendell respected the dashing captain and was quick to favor his plentiful suggestions. The Hackett crew, on the other hand, thought him arbitrary and overbearing. They did not like his mode of dress and deemed his braid and ruffles better suited for a masquerade than a ship's officer.

When it came to the clashing of ideas between Jones and James Hackett, Jones was the one who got his way, but often he found himself going for the compromise. Later, he was to realize that he owed a lot to Hackett. While true to Captain Jones's predictions that the *Ranger* would be hard to manage in rough seas, due to her long and heavy spars, she was a wild and beautiful ship before the wind.

Jones, the lover of ships, even knew how to make women feel loved and admired, but there is nothing recorded of him to indicate he ever singled out a particular one as the object of his affections. They served him as a means to an end and were, as he shrewdly detected, the ideal liaison between himself and any men in their lives whom he needed to cultivate. The captain was a willing social lion in what proved to be a dress rehearsal for his later appearances at the court of Louis XVI and his Queen Marie Antoinette of France.

When the ladies of Portsmouth flocked to Langdon's Island with picnics and parasols to behold their idol at work, he did not disappoint them. He gave them the performance they craved, darting hither and yonder giving orders with gentlemanly phrased commands couched in soft, well-modulated tones. He was having his cake and eating it too. If his conduct raised snickering doubts as to his abilities among the people of his building crew, he could set them to rights later. In the meantime, he was enjoying the role of celebrity, a pleasure he was never quite able to forego.

In private, before the men who were his sponsors, Jones sometimes gave vent to his irritations. He was bitterly opposed to the commissioning of privateers, an activity running wholesale on the northeast seaboard. Here he was touching a sensitive spot, for Portsmouth Harbor was a favorite anchorage for such government-commissioned ships, and there were many sponsors among his Portsmouth friends.

He was able to gain their sympathies when he pointed out that he had lost some of his most able seamen and officers among those who had sailed away on privateers and were now either lost or languishing in British prisons.

"Zealots! Zealots, all!" he cried. "Why could they not remain with a respecktable Navy?"

Why, indeed? Lost to him was Richard Dale, the impeccable officer from Virginia; Henry Lunt of Newbury, Massachusetts; and many other able seamen whom Jones himself had trained.

John Paul Jones permitted himself to be entertained by the leading families of Portsmouth. The ladies adored the handsome captain and held out their hands for his kisses. He was welcomed frequently at the home of John Wendell, who had a charming and eligible daughter. Her head was still in the clouds when the dashing captain put out to sea.

By the time the *Ranger* sailed, James Hackett and many of his builders were completely won over to Jones, and his outfitting of the sloop-of-war was accomplished in a manner to invite their admiration.

The *Ranger* was built for speed. She was flush-decked and constructed for the warfare of the day when it was ship-lashed-to-ship and man-fighting-man. Jones, not one to concede an issue, forever grumbled when her spars heeled in rough weather. But all was forgiven, and he would stamp the deck with glee when she switched and flaunted her stern at the frustrated enemy.

At such times, the *Ranger* was to him the most beautiful thing afloat, tempting a waste of shot, for with an east wind sweet and fresh abaft her beam, the Hackett-built ship was capable of unbelievable swiftness. Her coppered bottom low in the water, her top-heavy masts raking two or three degrees more than any other ship of the day, she was a fitting commission for a captain as daring as John Paul Jones.

The guns for the *Ranger* were made in America. Twenty-six had been provided, but Jones mounted only eighteen after deciding that more than this number would hamper action. Events of the future proved he was right in this. When the sloop-of-war was ready, her captain declared her the best ship he had ever seen and, in his characteristic master stroke of diplomacy, made the same declaration in favor of her crew. The *Ranger*'s complement consisted of men from many ports on the northeast seaboard, a large number from the Piscatauqua area. On their behalf, the nagging fault-finding Captain Jones complained to the Marine Committee that he "only had thirty gallons of rum for a crew of one hundred and forty-five men and officers."

The *Ranger* was ready to be put to sea, but no one ever would have guessed it. There was no sign of the crew, for it had been spirited aboard under cover of night a few at a time. The usual gala picnic took place on the day before departure to dampen any suspicion that such was in the offing.

With a tide and a wind to favor, Jones exercised his penchant for the unpredictable by having the *Ranger* launched without fanfare from the northwestern end of Langdon's Island, carrying what looked like a skeleton crew.

The flag *Ranger* flew from her masthead was a silken Stars

and Stripes made for the gallant captain by the ladies of Portsmouth. By this gesture, he carried with him all of their devotion. His friends, and even acquaintances, of Portsmouth were with him strongly to the end of his career, even after others had abandoned him.

In a record run, later described by awe-struck crew members as a circling course under full sail and at a speed sometimes terrifying to them, the *Ranger* arrived in France after thirty-one days at sea. In a letter to John Wendell from Nantes, Jones calmly wrote:

"After leaving Portsmouth, nothing remarkable happened until we drew Eastward of the Western Islands. Then, we fell in with Ships every day, sometimes every Hour."

When Jones left Portsmouth, he had with him one of the sons of John Wendell as a member of his crew. A rather florid description of the voyage to France is contained in a letter to Wendell from Jones, who wrote:

> The *Ranger* was wafted by the Pinions of the gentlest and most friendly of Gales along the surface of the Blue profound of Neptune; and not even the swelling bosom of a Friend's nor even an enemy's sail appeared within our placid Horizon until after we had passed the Everlasting Mountains in the Sea called Azores, whose Tops are in the Clouds, and whose Foundations are in the Centre. When, lo! This Halcyon Season was interrupted!
>
> The Fathering Fleets o'er spread the Sea and War's alarms began! Nor ceased they Day and Night until, aided by the Mighty Boreas we cast anchor in this asylum.
>
> But, wince, I am not certain that my Poetry will be understood, it may not be amiss to add by way of an original note that after leaving Portsmouth nothing remarkable happened until I got to the Eastward of the Western Islands; and from that time to my arrival here I fell in with Ships every day, sometimes every hour. Within eighty leagues of Ushant, I met with our enemy's fleet of Ten Sail bound up the channel.
>
> Notwithstanding my best efforts, I was unable to detach any of them from the convoy under which they sailed.

I met and brought too a variety of other Ships, none whereof proved British property except two Brigantines from Malay with fruit for London, which became prizes. The one is arrived here. The other, I am told, is in Quiberon Bay.

As I have met and brought too several Ships in the Night, I had the most disagreeable of proofs of the Active Spirits of my Officers and Men.

I have forwarded my Dispatches to Paris by Express and am determined not to go myself unless I am sent for.

I understand that in Obedience to Orders from the Secret Committee, the Commissioners had some time ago provided one of the finest frigates for me that can be imagined, calculated for thirty-two 24-pounders on one deck. [He's referring to the America.]

I understand that this ship is longer than any Ship in the enemy's fleet, but it has been necessary to give her up on account of some difficulties that they have met with at Court.

My heart glows with most fervent gratitude for this and every unsolicited and unexpected instance of the Favor and Approbation of Congress: and if a Life of Service devoted to the Interests of America can be made instrumental in securing its Independence, I shall be the Hapiest [sic], and regard the continuance of such Approbation as an Honor far superior to the empty Pageantry which Kings ever had the power to bestow.

I esteem your son as a promising and deserving young man. I have just now had some conversation with him and am much pleased with his diffidence and modesty. He would not, he says, accept a commission until he thinks himself equal to the duty of the office of Lieutenant. There I think he shows a true spirit. In the meantime, he tells me, he is perfectly Happy with his present Situation. Anything within my power to render his Situation Happy and Instructive shall not be wanting.

I must rely on you to make my Best Compliments acceptable to the Fair Miss Wendell and to the other agreeable ladies of my acquaintance in Portsmouth. . . .

The *Ranger* arrived in France on December 2, 1777, and Jones went on his devastating, but historic, cruise to the coast of Great Britain. This lasted until April, when, as was his hard and fast custom, he paused to restore and refit his ship.

They put to sea again that spring and succeeded to bedevil British commerce in the Irish Sea. Among other acts, they burned a brig off Cape Clear and made a daring descent upon the town and the shipping of Whitehaven. Sea coast residents quaked in their beds and were willing to impart any information to save their own necks. In this manner did Jones learn of the numbers of Americans in British coastal prisons. A daring scheme was devised. Born and reared on the estate of the Earl of Selkirk, Captain Jones thought it would be an excellent idea to capture the Earl and ransom him off in exchange for American prisoners.

Such a harum-scarum idea was never tried again by Jones, and it was, indeed, out of character for him to have attempted such a scheme in the first place. It failed for a very simple reason. The Earl disobliged his would-be kidnappers by not being at home when they called. Furthermore, Jones was extremely embarrassed when he learned that some of the *Ranger*'s men had stolen a large amount of silver plate belonging to the Earl. He lashed out at them in anger, "Do you not know," he cried, "that you have been guilty of an act of piracy?" It was an unwise choice of terminology, and it was promptly turned back upon Jones himself.

Charges of piracy were soon being leveled at John Paul Jones. Newspapers throughout England and some on the Continent were labeling him a renegade monster, acting without authority from any government. Back in America, liberal and Tory factions spread their verbal poisons. But before they could go very far, the agile Jones had accomplished another coup—this time a sea action. The *Ranger* fell in with the *Drake*, an English warship of superior crew and armament. The *Ranger* captured her and took her, a prize, into the harbor at Brest.

The Congress was immediately all forgiving and hailed the cruise of the *Ranger* a crowning success. It was not ready, however, to award Jones the acclaim he had earned. He was honest enough to admit that the Earl of Selkirk affair had hurt his established position.

## 15

## AFTER THE *RANGER*

When Benjamin Franklin broke the news to John Paul Jones that he was to be relieved of his assignment, the good doctor did not dissemble. He wrote: "You seem to be out of favor with Arthur Lee whose patrician ideas sometimes conflict with mine. I suggest that you come and spend some time with me. I am sorry, but you must give over the command of the *Ranger*."

Arthur Lee of Virginia was now American commissioner to France, but his dislike of John Paul Jones had begun long before. He had an able ally in that powerful statesman from Massachusetts, Samuel Adams. Between them, they made every effort to remove Jones from the American scene. Benjamin Franklin, however, who endorsed the controversial captain all the way, proved the greater strategist.

The conspirators thought that by having the *Ranger* returned to America they would have Jones out of Franklin's jurisdiction, but they counted without the skill of Franklin. He saw to it that the order for the *Ranger*'s return was carried out, but that Jones remained in France, Probably, this was the time when the plan for the formation of an American fleet on that side of the water came into being.

Jones was much chagrined, and he blamed his dilemma on the unfortunate attempt to kidnap the Earl of Selkirk. However, he was mollified to some extent when Franklin sought his advice as to whom they could trust to take the *Ranger* home. The former captain promptly selected Lieutenant Thomas Simpson of Portsmouth, New Hampshire, declaring that if he, Jones, couldn't have her, she should have only the best.

Simpson boarded the *Ranger* on Monday, July 27, 1778, after expressing undying gratitude and assuring Jones that he would always remember the lessons he had learned under superior tutorship.

John Paul Jones was still in fair favor with the American Congress. The members of the Marine Committee were delighted with the performance of the *Ranger*. They now were confident that the new frigate at Salisbury Point, Massachusetts, could do everything her sister ship had done, and more.

Jones, who had firsthand knowledge of the Hackett design, had reason to recall with favor the man who had introduced him to it, Henry Lunt of Newbury, Massachusetts. The captain's ire even softened to regret that he had sent Lunt away in harsh reprimand. Jones literally hungered after the new ship.

The treaty formulated between America and France in 1778* was the basis for naming the new frigate the *Alliance*, and Samuel Adams had a hand in it. The conservative Yankees of Salisbury Point who had built the ship did not like the name, nor did they approve of giving it to the command of a French captain, which is what happened.

John Paul Jones and Benjamin Franklin were delighted that the new frigate was to be called the *Alliance*, and they saw this gesture as one of supreme diplomacy to aid them in their activities on the other side of the water. All that was needed now was to accomplish the cartel exchange of British prisoners for American.

While the activities of Franklin and Jones during that period might seem to some to consist mostly of dawdling at the French court, the indomitable pair were actually engaging in a constant pulling of strings in the right places. They accomplished an amazing lot in so short a time, even stirring into action the phlegmatic and rather inert French Minister of Marine, M. Sartine.

When they had accomplished their first order of business in getting the *Ranger* to sea, she was carrying back to America needed supplies and several important letters of intelligence. The latter would result in the fullest cooperation of the Marine Committee, and in the activity against the British coastline that culminated in the famous *Bon Homme Richard-Serapis* sea fight.

Jones, with tears in his eyes, lowered from the *Ranger*'s masthead the silken Stars and Stripes made for him by the women

* See Appendix D, p. 215.

of Portsmouth. It later would fly during battle from the masthead of the *Bon Homme Richard.*

In France, while waiting for his new commission, it was impossible for Jones to ignore the social life, and it would be less than truthful to say that the gardener's son found it not to his liking. But his heart remained true to his ideals and his goals for an American navy to surpass that of Britain. He pressed for the cooperation the French government had promised. Foppish M. Sartine kept making proposals, mostly placating and going nowhere. In line with the politics of the situation, Jones kept making sounds of grateful praise while secretly looking elsewhere even higher. By the time Sartine and the jealous French officers discovered what the American captain was up to, much had happened.

Benjamin Franklin, American minister to France, was liked and admired by King Louis XVI, but he was adored by Queen Marie Antoinette and the ladies of her Violet Cotillion. Jones shrewdly decided that Franklin was the one who had the upper hand, in that he had convinced the French crown that America was a fast-rising power. Then, the captain received heartbreaking news.

Word came from America that the *Alliance* had been given to another—a Frenchman by birth, named Pierre Landais. The awarding of this commission to someone else was a bitter blow beneath the belt to Jones, one of many he was to suffer by this act alone.

Benjamin Franklin had succeeded in striking a cartel agreement was powerless in opposing equally powerful factions at home, rallied to the aid of his protégé. John Paul Jones received a commission, but it nearly broke his heart. Full of dismay and misgivings, he viewed his ship, the *Duras,* a large but old merchantman. Probably only Jones could have converted this wreck into a passable ship-of-war. He dared not seem less than grateful. In a gesture of good sportsmanship, he promptly gained permission to rename the *Duras* in honor of its sponsor. It became the *Bon Homme Richard* (The Good Man Richard) in a puckish I-don't-care attempt by Jones to reassure Franklin that his affection and esteem were still undying. Franklin was delighted with this recognition of his earlier literary gem, *Poor Richard's*

*Almanac*, and he caught the innuendo in the spirit intended. Jones, able to believe once more in his own indestructibility, prepared the *Richard*—as he was won't to call her—for sea, mounting forty-two guns.

Now, his old problem plagued him. How was he to find a crew for his ship? He needed at the very least 400 officers and men. As a start, he was forced to scare up about 150 men from all nations not interdicted by the laws of France. There he hesitated. He still believed the Americans would come from across the sea and from out of the British prisons. Again he had not underestimated his man, Franklin.

Benjamin Franklin had succeeded in striking a cartel agreement with England. Now, American prisoners could be exchanged for British. Jones was about to be reunited with some old friends.

A letter written by Benjamin Franklin tells of the cartel exchange of prisoners and gives some idea of how he brought it about. Franklin wrote:

> This cartel is at length brought about by the indefatigable endeavors of an old friend of mine, and a long declared one of America. He is a Mr. Hartley, a member of Parliament from Hull.
> The ship employed has already brought us one cargo from the prison at Plymouth [England] and is to continue. The Americans are chiefly engaged with Captain Jones and Captain Landais.

Franklin had been provided statistics to support his contention that prisoner exchange could provide a substantial increase of American seamen in the fleet of John Paul Jones. His intelligence told him that there were at least 354 men from off American ships in Old Mill Prison.

During the year 1778, the roll of Americans at Old Mill Prison continued to mount, but there were fewer and fewer attempts to escape. The reasons for this were elementary. As new prisoners arrived, they brought further word of home, and this alone made for a resignation and contentment of sorts. There was also a psychological inertia due to the fact that war news was not good.

June was a bad month in America. The evacuation of Philadelphia by General Clinton on June 18 was offset by General Washington's unsuccessful attack on Clinton's retreating columns on June 28 at Monmouth, where American forces were badly disorganized by the early retreat of General Charles Lee.

There were rumors that a peace pact was soon to be signed that would negate all of their past aggressions. British jailors were only too happy to inform their prisoners that Lord North had made conciliatory proposals which the Congress was said to be favoring.

The British Parliament finally had offered complete freedom from taxation except duties imposed for the regulation of commerce in exchange for peace.

The Americans at Old Mill were repeatedly approached and offered their freedom if they would sign up in the British navy. A depression settled over the prisoners, but only a few took the bait. Most refused to believe that America would surrender—nor did she. The British terms for peace were rejected, although the news of this was much later coming.

At that time, only Henry Lunt seemed to see a glimmer of hope and eventual freedom. He lost no opportunity to spread his belief about. From him, the prisoners were learning a lot about John Paul Jones, his incredible feats and seeming indestructibility. Their jailors were lending unwitting credence to Henry Lunt's reminiscences, although they didn't know it, when they railed at the Americans over their pirate captain who would soon swing from a yardarm.

But it soon became evident that John Paul Jones was not that easy to capture, and word of his daring exploits sifted into Old Mill Prison as new prisoners arrived.

The accounts, without a doubt, were grossly exaggerated, and the rumors that flew about were so extreme as to suggest that Jones and his marauders would soon storm Old Mill Prison and free its inmates. But some solid and believable intelligence also came through. The Americans knew with certainty that Benjamin Franklin was in France and had struck a treaty with that country.

The Lunt men, Henry, Cutting, and Richard, read more into the facts. They were elated and filled with pride to learn that the new warships were coming off the ways in New England shipyards. Here was honor and prestige to lift a man's chin and square his shoulders. The other American prisoners now were looking to the Yankee spokesmen and were being swayed by them. By the time Benjamin Franklin had made the cartel agreement with England for the exchange of captured British seamen for American, the prisoners of Old Mill were ready and willing to cast their lot with the indefatigable Jones.

Whatever sustaining influences permeated the foul atmosphere of Old Mill Prison, the days of 1778 were long and fraught with misery. Hardships persisted and food rations remained short. They could easily gauge the fluctuation of America's success and failure in the war by their punishments and persecutions. When their jailors were most harsh and ruthless, the prisoners could endure, rightly surmising that America had scored another victory. By the same token, spirits were dampened when the treatment they received improved, for it could only mean one thing—America had suffered another defeat on the battle line.

1779 was the year of deliverance, and events to bring this about were well under way in the last quarter of the year 1778. True to Henry Lunt's confident prediction, hundreds of Old Mill prisoners would follow the *Dalton*'s people into service in the fleet of John Paul Jones. First, to bring this about, the brave and beautiful little American frigate, *Alliance*, from Salisbury Point, Massachusetts, would bring to France, for exchange, British sailors from off the sunken warship *Somerset*. This thirty-two gun frigate was ordered to France to convey General Lafayette home.

Preparation for the *Alliance*, the second frigate completed by order of the Continental Congress, had commenced early in 1777, but building had not started until 1778 in the Webster Shipyard at Salisbury Point. Her builders were the brothers William and John Hackett, and she was ready for sea duty in July of that year.

The *Alliance* had everything the *Ranger* had, and more. She was larger; her tonnage 682. She was copper-bottomed; her bowsprit was long and low, built for speed. Jones later fussed and fumed about her, deploring the crowding of her decks with cannon. This very attention revealed how much he yearned after this beautiful ship-of-war.

The command of the *Alliance* had been given to Captain Pierre Landais, an ex-patriated French officer. This did not please the builders, nor did it please Commodore Jones, who lamented that "the best ship in the Navy had been given to a French officer." Jones appreciated the help given to America by France, but he was strong for an autonomous American navy working with, but not as part of, the French navy. Events proved that the French captain was not the man at first represented.

Landais arrived in America in 1775, and he struck up a friendship with none other than Samuel Adams, who claimed to disapprove of Jones because he had earlier engaged in slave trade. Adams pursuaded the Great and General Court of Massachusetts to make Landais an honorary citizen, hailing him as the navy's answer to the army's General Lafayette. On this wave of enthusiasm, it was easy for Adams to have his protégé made captain of the *Alliance*. The ship was ready, but there was difficulty in obtaining a crew.

In the first place, there were not enough able seamen left in the Newburyport-Amesbury area. Many were languishing in British prisons; the rest were assigned. There was a prejudice concerning service under a foreign officer who had not even mastered the English language. To overcome this difficulty, Massachusetts authorities resorted to impressment. Lafayette protested this move as against the principles for which they were struggling.

The authorities then agreed to Franklin's plan. They had in custody between seventy and eighty English seamen from the man-of-war *Somerset*, shipwrecked off the coast of New England the year before. The Massachusetts state government offered these men their freedom by exchange if they would serve aboard the *Alliance*, and they readily agreed. These men, a handful of French sailors and the rest Americans, made up the complement.

The *Alliance* sailed up to Boston and then left there on January 11, 1779. Lafayette was on board, and his friends worried. Their concern was justified, for a mutiny had been planned among the English sailors.

It was general knowledge that Parliament had passed a bill encouraging British sailors on American ships to mutiny. A substantial bounty was promised if they brought their ship to an English port.

The frigate had not been out many days when a conspiracy was begun. By the third week out, a plot had been well developed. The signal, "Sail-ho!" from the masthead at about daylight on February 2, was to call the mutineers to arms.

The mutineers were to form four divisions: one to clear the quarter-deck and kill any officer in sight; another division to secure the magazine; a third division to capture the ward room; the fourth division to seize the cabin.

The four long nine-pounders on the forecastle were secretly loaded with grape and canister and trained so as to sweep the afterdecks. All the officers, the surgeon, the carpenter and the gunners were to be killed. The lieutenants were to have a choice. They could navigate the ship to the nearest English port or walk the plank. The passengers, including General Lafayette, were to be turned over as prisoners upon arrival in England.

It seemed a workable plan. The date set for mutiny would be about two days from land to give the mutineers an advantage, but they were wise enough to know that they really needed the services of a skilled navigator. For this reason, they postponed the mutiny until four o'clock in the afternoon of February 2, instead of at daylight.

The mutiny was postponed for a practical reason, and it saved the ship. The mutineers had discovered a seaman who had unusual knowledge of navigation. They marked time while pursuading this man to join them. He was to serve as a safety measure in case the lieutenants refused to cooperate, or pulled a double cross by guiding the ship into a French port.

The mutineers thought the man they were dealing with was a native of Ireland because he had a brogue, but he proved to be an Irish-American. He pretended to cooperate until he had all of the details. He then informed the ship's officers.

Faithful crewmen were alerted. A few minutes after four, armed with fire arms and cutlasses, they rushed to the deck. The mutineers, caught unaware, yielded without a struggle. They were put in irons until the landing, at which time they were thrown into prison, later to be exchanged by cartel ship for American seamen.

After her arrival in France, the *Alliance* was placed in the squadron of John Paul Jones. The beautiful ship-of-war tore at his heart for sheer beauty of line. Here was the shape and design of the American battleship for years to come.

John Paul Jones and Pierre Landais struck sparks immediately when Jones complained of slack conditions aboard the *Alliance* and ordered her cleaned and rid of vermin. Landais declined. Things quieted for a time when the *Alliance* was ordered to Nantes, on the River Loire, where cartels were bringing in American seamen, prisoners-of-war for exchange.

The American Squadron* was established at L'Orient, a strongly fortified seaport at the head of the Bay Port Louis about three miles in from the ocean. It was ideal for the protection it afforded the ships of the fleet while preparing for the planned cruise to siege Liverpool.

Much to Captain Landais's avowed disgust, Jones was made the commodore of the fleet. Landais engaged in much chest thumping and many hysterical outbursts designed to reach the commodore's ears.

Fortunately, Jones heard little of it. He was too busy outfitting his ships, of which there were seven: three frigates, one corvette, one cutter, and two privateers. Jones gave little attention to the privateers, of which he heartily disapproved, and they did not long remain in his squadron.

Captain Landais challenged the right of Commodore Jones to head the expedition, declaring that he Landais, was the rightful commodore. Here was a situation Jones could not ignore in the interests of discipline.

Landais insisted that he, by virtue of a commission from America, had seniority over Jones, whose commission, according to Landais, had come from Dr. Franklin.

The truth was that Jones had received his commission from the Continental Congress long before when he was assigned the *Providence*. The commodore now had reason indeed to resent the mixup which had placed him eighteenth in seniority instead of sixth, where he rightfully belonged.

* See Appendix E, p. 218.

It was an unfortunate situation, and Jones was beginning to suspect that Captain Landais, with his sporadic outbursts and ever-changing moods, was afflicted with an ego-mania. He wrote to both Franklin and Lafayette confiding his just fears that Captain Landais would present an ever-mounting problem. However, there was nothing to do but go on.

The commodore had not long to wait before his troubles with Captain Landais came to the fore.

## 16

## THE CRUISE

At eleven o'clock on the morning of March 15, 1779, the gate of Old Mill Prison at Plymouth, England, swung open. Approximately 200 Americans, thin, bearded, and clad in rags, marched forth. Among them went 97 of the privateer *Dalton's* crew.

Later, Henry Lunt wrote to Sarah:

> There was a tear in every eye as, with heads still erect, we marched as best we could, admittedly a sorry and neglected crew. A few of our number we carried on litters, for we could not turn a deaf ear to their pleadings that they be counted as able men.
>
> It was two years and four months to the day from the moment of capture when we last breathed free air. Nor did we wholly comprehend that freedom until we felt beneath our feet the heave of the cartel's deck. We were still under heavy British guard.
>
> By the second day, we were fairly quartered, many of us lodging in cabins with beds of our own, and all of us with bedding to warm us some. The three or four sick among us were given single cabins by themselves.
>
> We were allowed the liberty of the deck by day and night, for our captors now knew with a certainty that none of us would try for escape.
>
> On the first day, we ate salt beef and pudding for our dinner, which some promptly give up over the side, their stomachs not being used to such fare. However, we soon made an adjustment to our varied diet which, although

better, was still no more in amount than prisoner's allowance.

Both officers and men of the cartel ship were more civil to us, a welcome change, as we waited in the Plymouth roadstead for a wind on which to sail. This did not come for nearly a fortnight, and, meantime, we learned that not all British are inhuman.

A Mr. Heath came among us with another of our friends, bringing for us wine, tea and sugar, which we had not tasted for too long. Mr. Heath also brought soothing medicine for our sick, which eased their groaning.

The very next day we were in mourning for one of our strong men who had suffered great punishment and privation. It was Bonner Darling, a Negro man who belonged to our *Dalton*'s crew. His death made the count twenty-one Americans who had died in our section of prison since being taken, and he made nineth to go of the *Dalton*'s crew.

When finally the wind came in good, we sailed out and were taken across the English Channel and down to Nantes on the River Loire. Then, there was some mix up with a delayed arrival of British seamen for exchange. However, in an even exchange, about fifty of us were released at once.

For the first time, us Lunts were separated, and cousin Cutting and I were reluctant to take our departure from his brother, Richard, who was forced to remain behind on the cartel ship.

Once on shore, we would have gladly kissed the ground and we were fairly met by friendly faces. We were immediately taken in tow by three fair seeming gentlemen who said they were from Benjamin Franklin who was representing us at the French Court. I shall never forget that moment of exaltation when I learned that Captain Jones was at a port on the French coast and had issued an invitation for all of us who would to join him on an American Navy ship.

The people practically tumbled all over each other to sign the enlistment papers, scarce hearing the terms we were offered. But, they did include a fair pay and a share of prize money. About forty of us signed for a twelve month of service and, with Cutting and me in the lead, set out with a guide to go overland to L'Orient, seventy miles to the north, where Jones awaited us. Some men, undecided, preferred to remain at Nantes, and a few we left to get word, if possible, to relatives and friends remaining on the cartel ship.

Never in my life would my mood be more jubilant, and I saw not only revenge for past suffering but an ignominious home coming turned into a hero's welcome. I resolved that Jones should give me an officer's berth, for I could serve him well once restored completely in strength. I had been assured that John Paul Jones, himself, would make us welcome. I determined to present my cousin, Cutting, as a better than ordinary person of the sea.

As we had hoped during the miles when our feet grew sore and blistered and we finally came to L'Orient, Jones welcomed us with undisguised joy. If he had an old grievance toward me for having left him for a privateer, there was no sign. He even expressed his condolences for our long and hard imprisonment and promised life would grow better for us with every day we served in the American Navy. It soon became evident, from our singling out, that cousin Cutting and I were to be put to good use. Richard Dale who, we then learned, had shared our incarceration in Old Mill Prison and had walked one day to freedom disguised as a British officer, was already made first lieutenant under Jones. He took us to the ship on which we would serve.

When we went aboard the *Bon Homme Richard*, Lt. Dale saw our dismay. It was an old, reconverted merchantman, a far cry from one of the new frigates on which we had thought to find John Paul Jones. That was when we learned that the frigate *Alliance*, originally promised to Jones, was now under the command of a Captain Landais. We did not waste time with idle regretting when we knew what a glorious mission the *Alliance* had undertaken. She was even then at Nantes with more than eighty British sailors saved from off the British man-of-war *Somerset* when she sank off the New England coast the year before. We recalled a coincidence in that we had watched the *Somerset* setting out on her last voyage from our prison ship in Plymouth Harbor.

Other British taken from prizes captured by Jones made the number on the *Alliance* for exchange around two-hundred men. This meant that our numbers would again be increased when the Americans were brought directly to L'Orient on the *Alliance*. They sailed from Nantes, without a hitch, on April 30th. Jones was in a rare, boistrous mood. Few of the exchanged Americans balked and, almost to a man, signed on with us in the American Navy.

John Paul Jones had an unfortunate brush with Captain Landais of the *Alliance*, who claimed some of our best people for his ship to make up for his loss of the *Somerset* sailors. Jones accounted this fair, but opposed Landais, in his reluctance to allow any of the reclaimed prisoners to sail with Jones on the *Bon Homme Richard*. Jones managed a better than even split by refusing to allow some of the men to return to the *Alliance* after signing with him for their enlistment. Cutting and I were sorely disappointed when cousin Richard Lunt and several others of the *Dalton* were among those caught in on the *Alliance*.

It was no time for bickering and Captain Jones prudently let the matter drop for the time being. There were other ships, and there was much to do. We were going on a cruise to scare the British and take as many of them prisoner as we could.

John Paul Jones summoned Henry and Cutting Lunt to the quarter deck. There, ceremoniously, with Richard Dale beside him, he made them officers of the United States Navy. The order in which they stood was as follows: Richard Dale, first lieutenant; Henry Lunt, second lieutenant, and Cutting Lunt, third lieutenant.

It was a disappointment that Richard Lunt had to serve on the *Alliance*, but it was also comforting to know that he and others of the *Dalton* would be able to keep close watch on the strange performance of their Captain Landais.

Orders came through which included the making of war on Liverpool in retaliation for the ravaging of the coast of Virginia by the British in May. The squadron set sail June 19, 1779, but they never got out of the harbor. Captain Landais, in the *Alliance*, performed like a novice at his first regatta and attempted to squeeze through the narrow strait at Port Lewis ahead of the *Bon Homme Richard*. The *Alliance* and *Richard* fouled, and in the contact, damage was done to both ships, which was assessed as follows: The *Bon Homme Richard* lost her head and cutwater, her spritsail yard and jib boom. The *Alliance* fared little better in that she had her mizzenmast carried away.

The Americans were mortified. The squadron returned to port, and the irate Commodore Jones invited Captain Landais to his quarter deck. It was Landais's only appearance there, and he came in the role of one who had been usurped of his seniority. He stood face to face with Jones in an attitude unbidden and shouted and ranted as one lacing down an insubordinate inferior.

When Landais, purple of face, paused to suck in a breath, Jones ordered the latter to return to his ship, and then, without pausing to determine whether his order had been obeyed, the commodore turned his back and walked in out of the weather. Landais had no other choice but to retire.

John Paul Jones at once notified Benjamin Franklin what had taken place, leaving out nothing. Franklin ordered an immediate private investigation, which came to nothing when it became evident that Landais would turn their scheduled cruise into a dry land debate of endless duration. As it was, repairs to both ships took longer than expected, and it was two months later, on August 14, 1779, after the British had ravaged the coast of Connecticut, that the expedition finally got underway.

In a month's time, the squadron of seven warships, all flying the American flag, had captured or destroyed twenty-six vessels and spread consternation along the coasts of Britain. Not since the days of the Spanish Armada had any nation so recklessly challenged the mistress of the seas. The Americans felt that Virginia and Connecticut were well avenged.

On August 18, a large ship belonging to Holland was captured. Upon boarding, it was discovered that she was in the hands of a British prize crew. Franklin, quickly notified, lost no time in acquainting the Dutch government with this perfidious British act. Therefore, British-Dutch relations, already strained, became tenser. This relationship came in handy for the Americans, however, when they needed a neutral port.

Captain Landais, never idle, gave his own orders, which were to the liking of Captain Guidloup of the privateer *Monsieur*. They took from the Dutch ship such prize articles as they wanted. Captain Guidloup put one of his officers in charge of the vessel, with orders to make for port.

When Captain Jones heard of this, he engaged in a successful testing of strength. Backed by his own officers and officers from the other ships, he was able to reverse Captain Landais's orders.

He sent the Dutch prize into L'Orient as agreed.

This angered the captain of the *Monsieur* who, having lost faith in Landais, enlisted the sympathies of the captain of the privateer *Granville*. The two separated their ships from the squadron on the evening of the following day, and they did not join up with it again.

On August 23, what was left of the squadron made Cape Clear. In the evening, while the Americans were chasing a brigantine in the vicinity of dangerous rocks off Ireland known as the Shallocks, the wind failed. This happening of nature could be called the turn of fate that spoiled the rapport existing between Henry Lunt and John Paul Jones.

The *Bon Homme Richard* was in peril of fouling on the rocks. Third Lieutenant Cutting Lunt was in charge of the operation to remove the ship from her position of danger. He lowered boats and sent them ahead with tow lines attached to the *Bon Homme Richard* to tow her seaward.

Cutting Lunt unwittingly appointed as coxswain in one of the boats an Irishman who had been flogged for a misdemeanor at L'Orient. That man selected six other Irishmen who, luke warm to the American's daring expedition, saw a chance to go home. They cut their tow line and rowed for shore.

Lieutenant Lunt, seeing them take off, resolved that they should not desert. Taking two other officers and nine good men with him, he lowered the jolly boat and went after them. The impetuous New Englander for once forgot to read his weather signs. A fog moved swiftly in, blanketing the coastline, and both boats were quickly engulfed—lost in the fog that hung all that night and the next day over the southwest Irish coast.

The next afternoon, while ships of the squadron remained powerless to move, Captain Landais went aboard the *Bon Homme Richard* and, without being announced, went straight to Captain Jones's cabin. He accused the commodore of losing boats and men in an attempt to take a prize. Landais was still acting as one appointed in command.

Jones, seething inwardly, acted the part of diplomacy while pointing out that the purpose of the expedition was to take prizes. He had nothing further to say, gritting his teeth through sheer force of will, and Landais was forced to retire.

In the late afternoon on August 24, with weather again clear, Jones sent the cutter *Cerf* to reconnoiter the Irish coastline and recover the missing boats and men. The rest of the squadron stood off a safe distance from the rocks. When the cutter failed to return by the next day, the squadron closed and ranged the coast. There was no sign of either boats or men.

It was later learned that the Irish deserters, familiar with their own coastline, had landed at Ballinskellix, County Kerry, where they immediately reported to the authorities that a boat load of Americans was following them. As a result, Third Lieutenant Cutting Lunt and his men were taken prisoner. Once again, he found himself in Old Mill Prison at Plymouth, England.

Commodore Jones was seething, but Second Lieutenant Henry Lunt was frantic. He was concerned for his cousin, and when it became apparent that those in the jolly boat were either drowned or captured, he grieved openly.

John Paul Jones made a possible mistake at this time. He turned on Henry Lunt and berated him, heaping on him full blame for the original order calling for tow lines "in a situation which probably would have righted itself."

Who was right or wrong in the matter probably never can be determined, but all suffered equally in a loss which took from the *Bon Homme Richard* nineteen men in all, three officers nine able seamen, and the seven Irish deserters.

Henry Lunt bore the brunt of the commodore's ire, and he was far more wounded by the public tongue-lashing than the work load now placed upon his shoulders. He accepted without a murmur the onerous task of dog's berth, previously accomplished by Cutting Lunt.

Henry, who loved to be up in the tops among the shrouds, had found Cutting a stimulating and challenging mate. The two together in their performances could give a show to excite the crewmen to follow and the officers to watch and applaud. All of this was over, for with Cutting gone the game lost its flavor for his cousin Henry Lunt. A pall fell over the sailor's routine.

The loss of Third Lieutenant Cutting Lunt was an important one, and not just because of the diminishment of their numbers. It marked the end of a mood of camaraderie that had existed between the officers and people of the *Bon Homme Richard*.

The failure of John Paul Jones in the matter was his seeming lack of compassion for Henry Lunt's personal loss. It was the kind of mistake the commodore seldom made, and as other problems crowded in and mushroomed, Jones put aside his displeasure and seemed to forget his antagonism.

But Lunt did not forget, and the wound to his spirit festered. While he applied himself without complaint to both his old and new duties, and did them as well and as efficiently as before, his mood was sour and melancholy most of the time. This feeling of discontent spread like a disease among the Americans, who were close to breaking under all they had endured and were always on the verge of homesickness. Where once Henry Lunt would have lingered in the shadow of his commodore seeking approbation, now, whenever he could, he sought, instead, the company of his elder cousin, Richard Lunt, and his former contemporaries of the *Dalton* who were still with Captain Landais on the *Alliance*.

Jones, when he learned of his second lieutenant's frequent trips over to the other frigate, was satisfied rather than annoyed. He knew the integrity of Henry Lunt, and he depended upon it—without disillusionment as things turned out. Despite his own disenchantment, Lunt remained loyal, and he reported on the peculiar actions of the *Alliance*'s captain. It was fortunate for Jones that he did in the light of subsequent developments.

On September 4, a pilot from the *Shetland* boarded the *Bon Homme Richard* and gave Captain Jones information necessitating a council of his captains. The signal to repair to the flagship was obeyed by all those present except Captain Landais. Captain Jones then sent several orders to Landais which went unnoticed. He then sent a written command to the captain of the *Alliance* which brought forth a disrespectful response. The council then proceeded without him. It was decided to make the third and last rendezvous and to complete one last search for the *Cerf*. That search proved fruitless. It was later revealed that the *Cerf* had returned to L'Orient.

Captain Jones stood down the eastern coast of Scotland, and during that time the *Alliance* sailed her own zig-zag course paying no attention to signals from the flagship. On Sept. 8, she disappeared altogether to the east. This left the *Bon Homme Richard* with only the *Pallas* and the *Vengeance*.

Captain Jones proceeded at sea, and land was not seen again until the afternoon of September 13, when the Cheviot Hills came into view.

On September 14, after maneuvering for a sloop-of-war of twenty guns in the Firth of Fourth near the city of Leith, a heavy gale carried them out to sea. Then, Captain Cottineau of the *Pallas* and Captain Ricot of the *Vengeance* began to create trouble.

On September 19, the *Vengeance* disappeared to the south in pursuit of several vessels. The *Pallas* followed with all the prizes, leaving the *Bon Homme Richard* all alone. However, on September 20, while skirting the Northumberland Coast, the flagship again fell in with the *Pallas* and the *Vengeance*.

Captain Cottineau reported that he had sunk one of the vessels he had chased the day before and that he had ransomed the prizes. This was against strict orders.

On September 21, the squadron engaged in much activity. By daylight it was noted that the *Pallas* had again disappeared.

The *Bon Homme Richard* and the *Vengeance*, sailing together, were now off the mouth of the Humber. Captain Jones headed north toward Flamborough Head where the *Pallas* had last been seen. During the night, two sails were chased, which, on the following day, turned out to be the *Pallas* and the *Alliance*. The *Alliance* had been absent for two weeks.

The reduced fleet was now sailing into danger and an historic encounter. On September 23, at noon, the American fleet was in action. Second Lieutenant Henry Lunt with sixteen men in the pilot boat was in chase of a brigantine and at least one hour away from the other ships of the squadron that were near Flamborough Head. As the American squadron came up from the south, a large sail, followed by others, rounded the Head from the north. Inside of twenty minutes, the Americans found themselves confronted by forty-two ships. It was not the most propitious moment for such a happening. Henry Lunt in the pilot boat received the signal for recall. When he could come about, he made a direct line for the American squadron.

Captain Jones raised his long glass and made a calm appraisal. He determined that only two of the ships were men-of-war acting as convoys. Then, as he watched, a boat pulled out fast from shore and drew up along side the larger British frigate, the *Serapis*. The bailiff of Scarborough went over the side to give notice of the American ships. Soon after, three little black balls ascended the mast of the *Serapis*. When they reached the masthead, they fluttered into signal flags, while, at the same time, a gun was fired to the windward. In this manner they signaled the presence of an enemy, and the merchant ships being convoyed scattered for shelter. The two frigates moved up to engage the Americans.

Everything was at stake. All now depended upon strictest attention to duty, the kind of disciplinary action for which Commodore Jones had long been in preparation. It is to be regretted that he was forced into battle under less than advantageous conditions, but the victory he accomplished was all the more remarkable because of this.

## 17

## THE BATTLE

In his preparations for the upcoming sea fight, nothing was going right for Commodore Jones. Captain Landais refused to put the *Alliance* astern of the *Bon Homme Richard* as ordered, and instead drew ahead. Henry Lunt was temporarily out of the picture, and Jones was left with only one experienced officer on the *Bon Homme Richard*, his First Lieutenant Richard Dale. Two others were with Lunt in the pilot boat.

It must be said for Captain Cottineau of the *Pallas* that he proved most gallant and brave. The action of the *Alliance* caused delay, and it was nearly dark before the *Pallas* could advance to engage the *Countess of Scarborough*, the other English frigate.

Landais, to the fury and frustration of much of his crew, remained aloof. Only rigid self-discipline kept these men at their posts awaiting the order to close once the *Bon Homme Richard* and *Serapis* grappled. That order never came. What was worse, it was surplanted by an order so incredible it is still hard to believe.

The furious battle that ensued has been written and studied, and there are few who omit the courageous words of Commodore Jones at the peak of battle. There was an hour of ferocious fighting. Then, with the two frigates lashed together, it became hand to hand. The *Serapis* had serious damage to her hull above the water line. The *Bon Homme Richard* was in worse trouble. She was leaking badly, and she had lost her battery of eighteen pounders. She now was relying solely on her twelve pounders.

Captain Pearson of the *Serapis* cast unbelieving eyes at the devastation all around. His situation was bad; he therefore shrewdly guessed that the Americans were in as bad, if not worse, trouble. He called out to the commander of the *Bon Homme Richard*, asking if he would surrender.

A stubborn resistence to defeat, ever to characterize the nature of John Paul Jones, brought about this defiant and historic response, "I have not yet begun to fight!" Then, inspired anew by his own oratory, the commodore gave the order that would turn the tide of battle in his favor.

A Scotsman named William Hamilton, a willing volunteer, crawled out on a yardarm carrying a basket of grenades and a live match. He ignited the entire basket and dropped it through a hatch into the gun room of the *Serapis*. There was a terrible explosion!

It was all over, and the Americans had won. Then Captain Landais, on the *Alliance*, performed an unbelieveable action. He attacked the *Serapis* and the *Bon Homme Richard* together.

There was never a way for Landais to explain what he did. In spite of the smoke of battle and explosion, the night was bright by a full moon and the phosphorescent glow from off the sea. The sides of the *Serapis* were painted yellow, and the sides of the *Bon Homme Richard* were painted black.

Captain Jones could not believe his eyes when the *Alliance* came into sight and fired a full broadside into the stern of the *Bon Homme Richard*. Americans on the *Alliance* later reported: "We asked him for God's sake to forebear, that he was killing Americans, but he passed on the off-side of the ship and continued firing."

Jones later wrote: "Every tongue cried out that he was firing into the wrong ship, but nothing availed. He passed around, firing into the *Richard*'s head and stern and broadside, and one by one his volleys killed several of my best men and mortally wounded a good officer on the forecastle."

A number of men had survived the battle while aiming telling shot, by gathering higher on the forecastle where enemy shot could not find them. The *Alliance*, in coming around the *Richard*'s bow, poured in a destructive fire of grape which killed or wounded twelve men.

In the meantime, Captain Pearson of the *Serapis* had struck. When it seemed in the confusion that the Americans would not honor his surrender, he hauled down the flag of Britain with his own hands.

The action of Landais was also ill-timed according to gentlemanly terms of surrender. During the last hour of battle, Henry Lunt and the sixteen men with him in the pilot boat came on the scene. Lunt tried desperately to size up the situation. It looked to him, at first, as if the *Bon Homme Richard* had struck. This was because the *Alliance* seemed about to take flight. She was running toward the *Pallas* and *Countess of Scarborough* that were still engaged in battle at a considerable distance to the leeward of the other two battling ships. The pilot boat moved in that direction.

Then, the *Countess of Scarborough* struck. A triumphant shout went up from the pilot boat as Lunt gave the order to move up to windward so that he might board the *Bon Homme Richard.* This was during the last of the battle. As they moved away, he noted that Landais was speaking the *Pallas.*

As Lunt was boarding the *Bon Homme Richard* on the offside, he became aware that the *Alliance* was abaft the *Richard*'s beam. However, he missed seeing the broadside that was allegedly fired by the *Alliance*, and he was too honest, later, to testify otherwise.

Landais, when later confronted, however, admitted the incident and boasted that he, and he alone, had caused Captain Pearson of the *Serapis* to strike.

When, immediately after the battle, Jōnes evaluated his situation, he was both appalled and dismayed. The *Bon Homme Richard* was an eerie sight to behold; she had holes in her hull so large that she seemed a skeleton ship out of legend. Her commodore wept as it became evident that she was foundering. She was already listing badly.

The Americans made every effort to save their gallant ship, and their British prisoners were only too glad to work with them in peril of their own survival.

The wounded received first attention, and all who would survive their wounds were placed aboard the *Serapis*. This took hours and strained the muscles of men already groaning after the furious sea fight. But they were to be further taxed. The call came from below that more men were needed on the pumps, and, exhausted though they were, all turned to and worked feverishly shoulder to shoulder. The situation was hopeless from the start, for the *Bon Homme Richard* was shipping water faster than they could pump it out.

Commodore Jones seemed impervious to their plight, and, although the men were dropping in their tracks, he drove them on. He desperately needed to save this ship for two important reasons: the decks of the other vessels were overcrowded, but more important to him, the *Bon Homme Richard* now had the prestige of a victorious man-of-war. It seemed he couldn't give her up, but he was forced to in the end.

Early in the morning of September 24, the commodore transferred his flagship to the *Serapis*. The pumpers knew then that their labors had been in vain and that they had lost the fight to keep the *Bon Homme Richard* afloat. They stuck with their post while as much as could be was salvaged and transferred to the other ship. After that, there was no time for the *Richard*'s crew to gather up their own belongings.

The last man hastened off the sinking frigate on the morning of September 25. He left none too soon. The ship settled rapidly, gave a heavy roll, and went down by her head into the German Ocean. It is said that she carried with her, badly tattered and torn but still proud and high on the masthead, the silken Stars and Stripes sewn for John Paul Jones by the women of Portsmouth, New Hampshire.

Commodore Jones had won a major sea battle; one to go down in history as a turning point in the decline of Britain's maritime might. Never again would the nations of the world tremble before her invincible navy. Governments of France and Spain rejoiced openly. The isles of Britain were in shock! America and France were in jubilation!

The hitherto invincible British navy had been struck a mortal blow from which she would never recover. What was worse, a British man-of-war had struck, not to a considered worthy adversary, but to a "converted merchantman in the hands of a motley crew." It was the talk of the colonies. It was the talk of all Europe.

The governments of Holland and Spain were secretly elated. Each offered sanctuary to the crippled American squadron.

The name of Commodore John Paul Jones was revered far and

wide as it never would be again, and it was to be short lived. For now, however, tongues that would label him pirate or corsair were temporarily stilled.

In the first days that followed his narrow victory, Jones remained unaware of the sensation he had created among governments of the western world. As a matter of fact, he could hardly believe that he had come away the victor in the *Bon Homme Richard-Serapis* fight.

When the commodore surveyed the ruinous condition of the *Serapis* from her decks jammed with both British and Americans, he was unable to achieve more than a cursory evaluation. Physically and emotionally exhausted, he did what human beings always seem to do. He turned on his friends.

Henry Lunt bore the brunt of his commodore's irascible humor. The loyal officer from Newbury, Massachusetts, tolerated this unfair burden with dignity, but he was even more resentful than before. Lunt felt he was not responsible for the tensions about him, and he lost no opportunity in transferring the blame to Captain Landais. In this, he had the support of his cousin, Richard Lunt, and others aboard both the *Alliance* and the *Serapis*.

Landais lost no opportunity (he, too, had spies) to point out that Henry Lunt had been no better than a deserter at the time of battle. Landais contended that Lunt had delayed in coming about in the pilot boat when he could have entered into battle and aided the *Bon Homme Richard*. He declared that he, Landais, was commodore and had given no order for the pilot boat to depart in the first place.

Lunt was placed in the embarrassing position of direct contradiction of a superior officer. The stoical New Englander, according to his rights, was caught no matter which way he turned. His position with Commodore Jones had been tenuous ever since his cousin, Cutting Lunt, had made the fatal error of being captured by the British. Jones still fumed over this and the loss of three ship's officers, nine men, and the jolly boat. Now, as he gazed upon the abject person of Henry Lunt, he was moved to blame him in spite of a long-placed confidence in the man Lunt and an opinion of no confidence at all in Captain Landais. There were only the men in the pilot boat to speak for Lieutenant Lunt, and they were not consulted until long after, when, at Corunna in Spain, Lunt submitted his resignation to Commodore Jones.

In the days following the *Bon Homme Richard-Serapis* fight, Jones seemed to have forgotten that it was he who sent Lunt and his men in the pilot boat after a prize. It did not matter at all that orders to return had been obeyed at once. The pilot boat had taken an hour to return, but as Henry Lunt explained:

> As we neared the scene of battle, we beheld the *Serapis* and the *Bon Homme Richard* locked in mortal combat.
> We then moved away, thinking we were the losers. Finding this not so as the *Countess of Scarboro* struck, we then moved up to board the *Richard*. We were forced to maneuver when, the *Alliance*, suddenly looming before us, cut the pilot-boat away, preventing our approach on the off-side.
> We saw not the grape-shot that took the *Richard's* fo' castle, but we witnessed a mad performance.
> We cried out in protest.
> By bright moonlight, we saw the *Alliance* rake grape-shot on both the *Bon Homme Richard* and the *Serapsi*.

Lunt later testified to this and to one other thing that was used against him. He had noticed that several guns on the *Alliance* did remain silent; officers and gunners either standing rigidly at attention or pressed against the rail crying out that their guns were killing Americans. Landais seized upon this and accused those who did not obey him of insubordination. He leveled charges that Jones had poisoned the minds of some key persons on the *Alliance*. The conniving Landais then went among his men, singling out those who had sailed with him from America to France and reminding them of their mutual courage in the face of mutiny. He sought out those Americans rescued from Old Mill Prison and told them not to forget that British seamen, brought from Boston on the *Alliance*, had been given in exchange for them.

Landais followed up by declaring a relaxing of duty and discipline, and he plied his men with choice viands and rum. Many of the men remained rip-roaring drunk all the way into port. Landais had won a point, but he now ruled a divided ship.

Jones, on the *Serapis*, had little time for politics. He watched and listened as best he could while dealing with first things first. He did appoint a commission to investigate the entire matter, but there was no time for attention to this until the squadron and prizes were brought safely into a neutral port. One thing was certain at that time, and the commodore knew it. He could not survive another major confrontation until his ships were repaired.

Although Landais claimed the title commodore of the fleet for himself, Jones was rightfully entitled to it. He was regarded commodore by the French court, which later even conferred its own equivalent on Jones.

Jones had more than his share of enemies and rivals, not only among his American contemporaries but also among scores of French officers seeking a high command who resented the attention paid the American officer. They complained that they were discriminated against while a foreigner went rewarded. Many of these were noblemen of wealth and were a constant source of embarrassment to the French ministry.

# 18

## AT THE TEXEL

The days following the fight were filled with discord and confusion. John Paul Jones was so tired he could hardly speak above a whisper. When he developed a fever, he yielded to the ship's doctor's plea and retired to bed in his quarters.

Surgeon Brooke of the *Bon Homme Richard* has described the commodore's voice as "still, soft, and small. He hated loud bawling." This factor influenced Jones greatly when selecting the officers who would be around him. His orders, in the midst of chaos, were carried out by Lieutenants Richard Dale and Henry Lunt, who understood his needs better than any. Lunt worried under the baleful eye of the commodore each time he approached the sick man, and he wondered, in human fashion, if his position had been completely undermined. There was little time for such conjecture. It was necessary to get under way before the English navy could gather its fleet for retaliation. They moved as fast as they could.

Jones had received orders that he should proceed to the Texel Island in Holland, the largest island in the chain that blocks off the Zuider Zee, seventy-five miles from Amsterdam. The commodore would have preferred Dunkirk, a free port and, by comparison to Texel, a short run to L'Orient.

In his flagship the *Serapis*, Jones sailed straight across the North Sea. Sick or well he obeyed orders, and it gave him extreme pleasure to be in command of a former British man-of-war—the first important prize ship taken by the American navy. Only three ships were left of his original seven. They were the *Alliance*, the *Pallas*, and the *Vengeance*. His most important prize, the *Countess of Scarborough*, was brought proudly along like a captive queen in chains. All of the ships' decks were crowded to capacity.

The *Serapis* was most desperately in need of repairs; something the New England craftsmen on the ship could handle once in port. Jones guided his squadron safely to the Texel roadstead by noontime or October 3, 1779. They had security for the moment in a neutral port. The sympathies of the Dutch government were with America, but the usual diplomatic complications were involved.

Commodore Jones, somewhat recovered, looked over the situation and made a minute examination of his ships. The *Serapis*, which he had concluded would continue to be his flagship, was his first concern. He managed to secure the services of some Dutch workmen to augment his own skilled carpenters and riggers. As was to be expected, he had trouble with the Dutchmen, who found him too exacting and fault-finding. For once, he made no effort to exercise his charm. Commodore Jones was in a foul mood from which he did not completely recover until many weeks later when he was once again at L'Orient.

Franklin wrote to Jones in a letter dated October 15, 1779, informing the commodore that all of Paris and Versailles were praising his courage and valor in the *Serapis* fight.

Concerning Captain Landais, Franklin wrote: "I know not whether Landais will obey my orders nor what the ministry will do with him; but I suspect they may, by some of their own concise operations, save the trouble of a court-martial."

Nevertheless, the good doctor had written to Captain Landais informing him that he would have the opportunity to answer to charges of disobedience of orders and neglect of duty. Franklin, a shrewd judge of men, had no faith in the French captain, and considering events of past and succeeding months, his opinion was justified.

Jones, somewhat mollified by Franklin's praise, was riled again in the next instant to learn he was to be deprived of his flagship. The *Serapis* and the *Countess of Scarborough* had been given to France, which had already reclaimed the *Vengeance*.

The *Alliance*, in deplorable condition, was given to Jones, and he had to start all over again to bring about a tight and workable ship. First, he had to maneuver Landais out and himself aboard.

Captain Landais was in disgrace. An accusatory document was drawn up and signed by an imposing number of officers on all ships. Under orders from the commodore, his officers were assigned the laborious task of obtaining the signatures before the squadron broke up. Despite being worn out from the irascible temperament of Jones, Henry Lunt again came through and did his part. The result was a damaging list of accusations against Captain Landais by many officers of the squadron.

This well-guarded paper has been preserved, but it had little or no influence when the court-martial of Captain Landais was eventually held. In spite of all that Benjamin Franklin could do, the court-martial was delayed and not held until the following March after the *Alliance* had returned to America. But then, those who had issued signed statements were scattered far and wide.

The document* reads as follows:

Certificate of a Number of Officers
Respecting the Conduct of Captain Landais

We the Officers of the American Squadron now at *The Texel*, this 30th Day of October, 1779, do attest and declare on our Words of Honor as Gentlemen; that all of the following Articles which We Subscribe respecting the Conduct of Peter Landais, Captain of the Frigate *Alliance*, are really and truly matters of fact in Witness whereof We hereunto Sign our Names and Qualities; and will at any time hereafter be ready to prove the same upon Oath if required:

1. The Captain of the *Alliance* did not take the Steps in his power to prevent his Ship from getting foul of the *Bon Homme Richard* in the Bay of Biscay; for instead of putting his helm a Weather and bearing up to make way for his Commanding Officer (Which was his duty) he left the Deck to Load his Pistols.

2. When in chase of a Ship (Supposed an English Indiaman) on the -- Day of August, 1779, Captain Landais did not do his utmost to overtake that Ship which he might easily have

---

* See Bibliography, item 8.

done before night; but put his helm a Weather and bore away several times in the day after the *Alliance* had gained the Wake of the Chase and was overtaking her very fast.

3. Captain Landais behaved with disrespect and impertinence toward the Commander-in-Chief of the Squadron on frequent occasions.

4. He disobeyed his Signals.

5. He very seldom answered any of them.

6. He expressed his Fears and Apprehensions of being taken on the Coast of Ireland, and insisted on leaving sight of it immediately when we had cruized there only two Days.

7. His Separation from the Squadron the first time must have happened either thro' ignorance or design, because tho' he distinctly saw the Signal for the Course before Night met, he Altered it first two and then four points of the Compass before morning.

8. His Separation from the Squadron the Second time must also have happened thro' Ignorance or Design, because the Wind being at N.W. and the other Ships to His knowledge laying too and being a Stern of the *Alliance*, what less than a Separation could be the Consequence of his Obstinacy in Ordering the Weather main brace to be Hauled in and the Ship to be Steered S.W. and S.W. by S. in the Trough of the Sea; which was done from ten at Night 'til Morning; and he would not then permit the Ship to be tacked in Order to rejoin the Squadron as was proposed to him by the Officers.

9. On the Morning of September 23d, when the *Bon Homme Richard* after being off the Spurn came in sight of the *Alliance* and the *Pallas* of Flamborough Head, Captain Landais distinctly told Captain Cottineau that if it Was as it Appeared a Fifty-gun Ship, they must run away: altho' he Must have been Sure that the *Pallas* from her Heavy Sailing must have fallen a Sacrifice.

10. In the Afternoon of the same Day, Captain Landais paid no Attention to Signals, particularly the Signal of Preparation and for the Line which was made with Great Care and very Distinctly on board the *Bon Homme Richard.*

11. Altho' the *Alliance* was a Long Way ahead of the *Bon Homme Richard* when bearing down on the Baltic Fleet, yet

Captain Landais lay out of gun shott to Windward, until the *Bon Homme Richard* had passed by and Closely engaged the *Serapis*, and then instead of Coming to Close Action with the *Countess of Scarborough* the *Alliance* fired at very long Shott.

12. He continued to Windward and a Considerable Time after the Action began, fell a Stern and Spoke the *Pallas*; leaving the *Countess of Scarborough* in the Wake of the Ships engaged and at free Liberty to Rake the *Bon Homme Richard*.

13. After the *Bon Homme Richard* and the *Serapis* were made Fast along side of each other, as in the Margin (which was not Done untill an Hour after the Engagement began) Captain Landais, out of musket shott, Raked the *Bon Homme Richard* with Cross Bar and Grape Shott which killed a number of men, dismounted Sundry guns, put out the Side Lights and Silenced all the twelve-pounders.

14. The *Alliance* then ran toward the *Pallas* and *Countess of Scarborough* that were at the time engaged at a Considerable distance to Leeward of the *Bon Homme Richard* and *Serapis*, and Captain Landais hovered there out of Gun Shott and without Firing 'till some time after the *Countess of Scarborough* had *Struck*, and then bore down under his Topsails and Spoke first the Prize and then the *Pallas* asking a number of Questions.

15. At last Captain Landais made Sail under his Topsails to Work up to Windward, but made his Tacks before he (being within Range of Grapeshott and at the Longest three-quarters of an Hour before the *Serapis* Struck) fired a Second Broad-side into the *Bon Homme Richard*'s beam, altho' many Tongues had Cry'd from the *Bon H. Richard* that Captain Landais was firing into the wrong Ship and pray'd him to lay the Enemy along-side. The three large Signal Lanthorns with proper Signal Wax Candles in them and well lighted had previously to his Firing been hung over the Bow, Quarter and Waist of the *Bon H. Richard* in a horizontal Line, which Was the Signal of Reconnaissance, and the Ships, the One having a Low Stern with Yellow sides, were easily distinguishable, it being a Full Moon.

16. The *Alliance* then passed at a very Considerable distance along the Larboard or off side of the *Bon Homme Richard* and, having tacked and gained the Wind, ran down again to the Leeward and, in Crossing the *Bon H. Richard's* bow, Captain Landais raked her with a third Broadside after being Constantly Called to from the *Bon Homme Richard* not to fire, but to lay the Enemy along Side.

17. Sundry men were Killed and Wounded by the Broadsides mentioned in the two last Articles.

18. Captain Landais never passed on the off-side of the *Serapis*, nor could that ship ever bring a Gun to bear on the *Alliance* at any time during the Engagement.

19. The Leaks of the *Bon H. Richard* increased much after being fired upon by the *Alliance*; and as the most dangerous Shott which the *Bon H. Richard* received under water was under the Larboard bow and the Quarter they must have Come from was the *Alliance*, for the *Serapis* was on the other Side.

20. Several people on board the *Alliance* told Captain Landais at different times that he fired on the Wrong Ship. Others refused to fire.

21. The *Alliance* only fired Three Broadsides while within Gun Shott of the *Bon H. Richard* and *Serapis*. ·

22. The morning after the Engagement, Captain Landais acknowledged on board the *Serapis* that he Raked each time with grape Shott which he knew would scatter.

23. Captain Landais has acknowledged since the Action that he would have thought it no harm if the *Bon H. Richard* had Struck, for it would have given him an Opportunity to retake her and to take the *Serapis*.

24. He has Frequently declared that he was the only American in the Squadron, and that he was not under the Orders of Captain Jones.

25. In Coming into The Texel, he declared that if Captain Jones should hoist a broad pennant he would, to Vex him, hoist another.

The signers of the above document were encouraged to read

the charges carefully before affixing their signatures. As a result, here is an opportunity to see how on-the-spot observations can vary with the individual. They attested as follows:

I Attest the Articles Numbers 2, 3, 4, 5, 6, 10, 11, 13, 15, 16, 17, 19, 21 & 22 to be matters of fact and I believed all the Rest.
J. W. Linthwate, Midshipman of the late *Ship Bon Homme Richard.*

I Attest the Articles Numbers 2, 4, 5, 10, 11, 15, 16 & 22 to be matters of fact and I believe all the Rest.
Robert Coram, Midshipman of the late *Ship Bon Homme Richard.*

I Attest the Articles Numbers 2, 3, 4, 5, 6, 10, 11, 13, 15, 16, 17, 19, 21 & 22 to be matters of fact and I believe all the Rest.
John Mayrant, Midshipman of the late *Ship Bon Homme Richard.*

I Attest the Articles Numbers 1, 2, 3, 4, 5, 6, 7, 8, 10, 15, 16, 17, 18, 19, 20, 22, 23 & 24 to be matters of fact and I believe all the Rest.
Lt Colo Wubert, American Engineer and Commanding Officer of the Volunteers on board the *Serapis*, late of the *Bon Homme Richard.*

I Attest the Articles Numbers 2, 3, & 11 to be matters of fact and I believe all the Rest.
Benj[a] Stubbs, Midshipman of the late *Ship Bon Homme Richard.*

I Attest the Articles Numbers 2, 3, 4, 5, 6, 10, 11, 13, 15, 16, & 17 to be matters of fact and I believe all the rest.
Thomas Potter, Midshipman of the late *Ship Bon H. Richard.*

I Attest the Articles Numbers 2, 3, 4, 5, 10, 11, 13, 15 & 19 to be matters of fact and I believe all the rest.
Nath[l] Fanning, Midshipman of the late *Ship Bon Homme Richard.*

I Attest the Articles Numbers 3, 4, 5, 10, 11, 13, 15, 16, 17, 19 & 21 to be matters of fact and I believe all the Rest.

Tho[S] Lundy, Midshipman of the late *Ship Bon H. Richard.*

I Attest the Articles Numbers 2, 3, 4, 5, 6, 10, 11, 13, 15, 16 & 17 to be matters of fact and I believe all the Rest.

Beaumonte Groube, Mid[n] of the late *Ship Bon Homme Richard.*

We Attest the Articles Numbers 2, 3, 4, 5, 7, 8, 11, 12, 18, 20 & 21 to be matters of fact

NB The *Alliance* never  James Degge, Lt.
passed on the offside of  John Buckley, Master
the *Serapis* -  John Larcher, Mast[r]. Mate.

I Attest the Articles Numbers 2, 3, 4, 5, 10, 11, 15, 16, 17, 18 & 23 to be matters of fact.

Stack, Lt., of Walsh's Regt & Officer of Volunteers on board the *Bon Homme Richard* by Congé from Court

I Attest the Articles 2, 3, 4, 5, 6, 10, 11, 13, 15, 19, 23 & 24 to be matters of fact.

McCarthy, Off[r] of Walsh's Regiment and Lieut. of Volunteers on board the *B. H. Rich*[d]

J'atteste les Articles n. 12, 14 et 24 quant a L'article 4, j'ai connoissance qu'il a refuse' d'obeir aux Signaux de Serendre a bord du *Bon Homme Richard*, et relativement a L'article 9. Je me rappelle qu'il me dit, Si C'est un Vaisseau au dessus de 50 Cannons, nous n'avons plus que le parti de la fuite.

Signe D Cottineau De Kloguene
Cap[e] de la *Pallas.*

I Attest the Articles Numbers 2, 5, 11, 12, 20 & 22 to be matters of fact.

M Parke Capt[n] of Marines on board the American Frigate *Alliance.*

I Attest the Articles 2, 3, 4, 5, 15, 16, 17, 18, 19 & 21 to be matters of fact.

Richard Dale Lieut of the late Ship of War the *B. H. Richard.*

I Attest the Articles Numbers 2, 3, 4, 5, 11, 14 & 22 to be matters of fact.

Henry Lunt, Lieut of the late *Ship Bon Homme Richard.*

I Attest the Articles Numbers 2, 3, 4, 5, 10, 11, 13, 15, 16, 17, 18, 19 & 21 to be matters of fact.

Samuel Stacy, Master of the late Ship the *Bon H. Richard.*

## 19

## FLAGSHIP *ALLIANCE*

Captain Landais had been offered no new commission. He was nearly insane with wrath. While admitting most of the charges leveled against him, he could see no insubordination in his conduct. In his own mind, he, and not Jones, was in command of the squadron and had always been.

The more serious charge of treason he swept away. He saw nothing preposterous nor treasonous in having ordered the *Alliance* to fire upon the *Bon Homme Richard*, "a French ship under the command of a pretender" who had usurped the prerogatives of an American ship.

Landais ranted and raved until he had whipped himself into a fighting frame of mind. Not ready to take on Jones, he cast his eye around for an adversary he could probably best, thinking to reestablish a rapport with the people of the *Alliance*. He settled on Captain Cottineau, to whom Jones, ever faithful to his duty, had yielded the command of the *Serapis*.

Captain Landais challenged Captain Cottineau to a duel. Cottineau, young and a gentleman, could have washed his hands of the entire affair and sailed away with his honor intact, but the chivalrous Frenchman could not ignore the challenge. The duel was fought, and Landais, an expert swordsman, came off best. He inflicted a deep and lasting wound that caused endless suffering for the vanquished Cottineau.

Considering his less than admirable position, whether he knew it or not, Captain Landais might have taken the advice offered him by Benjamin Franklin—"to quit before he had both feet in the mire." But the obviously mad Landais considered his win over Cottineau a major victory. He then went a step farther and challenged Commodore Jones to a duel.

Jones had other ideas on what constituted chivalry, and he immediately sent an officer to arrest his challenger. Landais had not counted on this. Crying out that Jones was no gentleman, he took off for Paris so precipitately that he left most of his belongings behind him on the *Alliance*. Upon his arrival in Paris, he explained his about-face and hasty departure by declaring that the "wild corsair" had threatened to hang him from a yardarm.

John Paul Jones was over his head in activities vital to survival, or he surely would have seen to it that Landais's possessions followed him straight away. The commodore was to regret that he had not attended to that small detail. The fracas with Captain Landais was but a sidelight in the affairs of international diplomacy that now plagued Jones. On the brighter side was the acclaim directed toward Jones for having scored a victory in a major naval battle.

In America, Commodore John Paul Jones was ordered a citation by Congress. In France, preparations went forward to pay him highest honors at the court of King Louis XVI. Informed of all this by letter from Dr. Franklin and the Marquis de Lafayette, Jones wrote to Lafayette on October 28, 1779: "I never meant to ask a reward for my services, either in France or America. Consequently, the approbation of the Court and of Congress is all the gratification I can wish for."

From France, Benjamin Franklin did everything he possibly could to encourage John Paul Jones during the dark and spiritless days in Holland when the commodore was practically without funds and surrounded by embarrassments.

He never knew from one day to the next when the Dutch faction wanting him out of the Texel would gain a majority over the one permitting him to stay. If forced out too soon, he would surely fall prey to the large British fleet lying in wait for him on the sea. This seesaw position was nerve wracking.

There was the immediate question as to how the prisoners from off the prize ships were to be conveyed to France without recapture. Franklin, in a letter to Jones, dated October 15, 1779, wrote: "I am uneasy about your prisoners. I wish they were safe in France. You will then have completed the glorious work of giving liberty to all Americans who have so long languished for it in British prisons, for I think possibly there are not so many there as you have now taken in prisoners."

The beautiful frigate *Alliance* was in a deplorable state. Captain Landais, who never bothered with maintenance, had really neglected her. Her sails were ragged, her cables in decay. Her small arms were out of order and most of her powder was damaged by leakage. Nobody had bothered to turn the kegs, a very necessary and routine procedure. Many of the people of the *Alliance* were intemperate and dirty and inclined to insolence. Her officers were, in the main, as insubordinate as their former captain, and they quarrelled among themselves.

Discouragement heaped upon discouragement, but Commodore Jones, aided by his subordinate and well-trained staff, went doggedly forward. Jones, always a devoted admirer of a slick sailing ship, intuitively knew the *Alliance* as he had known her smaller sister-ship, the *Ranger*. As for his New England contingent, the yards of these ships were more familiar to them than the streets back home.

In an all out effort to repair the *Alliance* as quickly as possible, officers as well as men turned to with a desperation borne of fear of capture rather than good will. They were favored in this instance by a spell of bad weather that kept the British squadron far off shore. Pressures on the Dutch by the British to drive Jones out of Texel were temporarily eased.

The *Alliance* was re-rigged and careened; her bottom was scrubbed. When done with their feverish efforts, she was far from what Jones deemed that she ought to be, but she would do.

The commodore trusted the proud *Alliance*, and she soon justified his trust. Under his command, and in the hands of the ablest seamen in the world, she flew like the true American eagle that she was before the mighty British fleet. Not one of the pursuing ships could even come up with her.

The fierce storm was abating. The Dutch government, goaded by the British, finally ordered the Americans out.

Jones was as ready as ever he would be. He was sick of being called a corsair by his French detractors and pirate by the British. When the French ambassador thought to save his skin by offering him a letter of marque as captain of a privateer, Jones exploded. He would leave Texel, and he would show them all!

He received the order to leave around November 17. The

*Alliance* now had a picked crew of 427 men, the cream of the late *Bon Homme Richard* as well as the *Alliance*. Nearly all were Americans but there was a problem among them: the men who had not sailed under Captain Jones directly were not accustomed to his relentless insistence upon order and discipline.

They made ready to go while pretending to stay. Prior to sailing, Commodore Jones appeared before his full ship. He was calm, and his voice, soft and musical, could be heard by all. When standing on the quarter deck above them, he always seemed taller to his men than he actually was. This was one of the few occasions when his entire crew was with the gallant captain. He was pale—the freckles on his face standing out boldly—and his eyes were the green of the sea. Something of his amazing courage seemed to transfer to them, Henry Lunt said later, as he told his officers and people that a large British fleet was waiting to pounce on them off the Texel Island. He impressed upon them that he would never shirk an engagement with any English ship mounting up to fifty guns.

Jones was ready to go! He sent formal word to the Dutch officials he would leave when the wind permitted.

Prior to sailing, one cheering bit of news came from Benjamin Franklin. The good doctor had succeeded in obtaining liberation of all American prisoners in England by exchanging them for the prisoners captured by the commodore. So many British prisoners had been successfully removed from Holland, that England would receive the equivalent and possibly more men than she would be able to deliver to the American side.

A severe storm had scattered the British ships out to sea. John Paul Jones watched for the first break in the weather. Never was a leader more tested and found true as was the commodore at this time. His squadron had been dispersed; he was commander of one ship only. He could trust barely half of his crew.

With nothing but his instinct and his rigid adherence to duty to stand him in good stead, he trembled on the brink of failure and what looked like certain capture. However, like a benediction from heaven, the elements were with him, and he knew how to capitalize. On December 26, 1779, the day after Christmas, the wind came in fair over rough seas.

The British signalmen were at ease, convinced that their fleet had ample time to re-form its blockade. Then, at midnight, before the British could realize what they were about, the Americans went into action.

The French ambassador to Holland had ordered that henceforth only the French ensign could be flown from all ships, including the American. This was an insult neither Jones nor any American could accept. They paused only a moment for a little ceremony. Seriously and revently, in total silence, hats lifted high in tribute, they raised their own American colors. Then Jones rigged a springline on a second anchor to get the wind into his sails, and he cleared the land. With the wind abaft her beam, and every inch of her canvas spread, the *Alliance* fled into the dark of early morn. The flight began on December 27, 1779.

Back in Salisbury Point, Massachusetts, those master builders, William and John Hackett, their carpenters and joiners, caulkers and painters, tinmen and all the rest, sat in the dark of a winter evening before the blazing hearths of home. Ice lay thick upon the Merrimack River, and snow banks glistened whitely along the shore. As they nodded by the warmth of their fires, did they dream of the beautiful frigate they had built to their own design with their own hands? Did they wonder where she was and how she fared? It is a pity they could not have seen her as she fulfilled their every expectation, skimming along the sea at an incredible speed all the way within sight of the Flemish shore—a sizeable British fleet in distant pursuit.

The escape from the island of Texel has been hailed as one of the greatest naval maneuvers in all history. Due honor has been paid to John Paul Jones. It was Jones himself who extended that honor to include his valiant crew.

It was early evening in New England but after midnight on Texel when the *Alliance* began her flight. Before morning, the masterful Commodore Jones had her far down on the German Ocean. Keeping well to windward of the enemy fleet, Jones sailed the *Alliance* down the North Sea and through the Straits of Dover in full view of the English fleet in the Downs. He passed the Isle of Wight within cannon shot of shore. The British had no choice but to swallow defeat and humiliation as the "inferior pirate" they had sworn to hang outsailed and outsmarted them.

Jones eluded them all, safely emerging from the English

Channel and continuing on his course down the western coast of France. His voyage covered, altogether, about 1,500 miles. It ended at the port of Corunna in Spain. Some have questioned the rightness of a visit to Spain at that time, but, in so doing they have neglected to look at the diplomatic situation. It was, in the opinion of Dr. Franklin, a most propitious time for such a visit, for the proud British had suffered a put-down, and Spanish-American relations were on the up-swing.

Spain, in those days, owned Louisiana, a province extending from New Orleans up through St. Louis. Spain had declared war against England the previous summer on July 8, 1779. Since that time, she had been assisting America with money and supplies all up and down the Mississippi River.

When British forces launched a large attack on St. Louis in 1780, the Spanish forces were waiting for them. They clashed and fought in what is now referred to as the Battle of St. Louis. The Spaniards won.

Dr. Benjamin Franklin was the supreme diplomat, and he had absolute faith in his protégé John Paul Jones. It was intelligence from Franklin which directed the hero of the hour to Spain at a time when a jealous reaction from the French court was least likely. As the eminent doctor wrote, "The celebration in France will be twice as sweet for the waiting."

From the standpoint of practical politics, Jones agreed, but from a personal standpoint, he must have differed with his mentor. The commodore was ailing, and he was bone tired from lack of rest. While allowing that his men probably felt the same, he still drove them relentlessly.

As for Second Lieutenant Henry Lunt, he had reached the breaking point. He was so far into the doldrums of discontent, he no longer cared who knew it. Lunt wrote a letter home in which he declared his intention of resigning from naval service "as soon as ever I can." He also described the flight from Texel most dramatically. The pertinent parts of his lengthy letter follow:

> When we arrived at *The Texel*, we were received well enough by the Dutch, but it didn't last.
> When we boarded the *Alliance*, we were disgusted with the shape she was in. The pretty frigate was filthy and

neglected, testifying to the sloppy seamanship of Captain Landais. He had left her armament and equipment deteriorating and her hulk fouled. Her people were a motley sight and no credit to an American Navy, many of them drunken and insubordinate.

There was trouble, as might have been expected, with the two crews, from *Alliance* and *Serapis* put together. I had trouble convincing my own obedient seamen that they should help to repair and clean a ship they had had no part in fouling up. But, they are good lads, accustomed to taking orders, and they did turn too.

The Commodore was more disagreeable than ever, and I could not wholly blame him. What I could and did blame him for was that it always began and ended with me. It seemed to matter not if we stood before or away from the people. I often consulted Lieutenant Dale as to what I could do or where he thought it all would end—for I would sooner go on my own than be asked to resign.

I hoped that the Commodore's disposition toward me would improve once we were out of *The Texel* and at sea, but such was not the case. If anything, it worsened. His jibes toward all of us by name of Lunt were more than I could bear—him forever and always blaming me for my cousin Cutting's unfortunate disappearance off the Irish coast.

When we went from *The Texel*, it was in the dark of the morning on December 27 with a good wind to the East, under our good American colors—for if we were to be taken it would be under no other flag.

In rough seas at noon on the 31st December we cleared the English Channel, still running free. The run out of *The Texel was one no man among us will ever forget. It was a race for our very lives, and we all knew it*. Not even the least of the people shirked due to the fear that drove us from without and within. From the standpoint of performance, it was a highly successful cruze. I am driven to admit that I, as well as the rest, was proud of our Commodore. None was ever braver or more daring before or since. He showed our heels to the British.

Although I did my duty as well as usual, the Commodore's

acquired habit of blaming me for everything did not subside. I was up in the yards or at the wheel a good share of the time, always taking direction from the Commodore himself. It was outrun the British or swing from a yard-arm, that we all knew. I could see the terror in the faces of the men about me, and terror was tight in my own throat, yet, my will and my hands obeyed like a well-trained puppet obeys a supremely skilled puppeteer.

This, then was the outcome of practice, endless practice, until a man could drop in his tracks. Jones beat at me from above, beside and behind. He was here, there and everywhere as was his custom. His eyes blazed at me like two flashing green starboard lights, and his tongue was a lash which whipped and stung me.

"Ho, Lunt," he sneered in my very ear, "Let's see that seamanship you brag of—or will you be the first to hang. If I have my way, and we are caught, that you will—you shirker from the *Richard* fight. Hold her steady, you blithering fool, or we heel and go over."

And, so it went. This was cruelty of the meanest part to me, who anguished even yet over absence from the *Serapis-Bon Homme Richard* battle. Always before, when we gloated of our victories and prize taking, I had been strongly in it. That was over, and now it was only Richard Dale who had the Commodore's praise. But, Lieutenant Dale I will not put down. He is a brave and skillful officer.

Of such was my resentment in that mad run for safety out of *The Texel*, it overrode my fears. Besides, my task was hard, calling for all that human strength could give. I had to call for many hands at once to steady the wheel, so hard did she kick, and the wind was like a demon worrying our sails until our ears went deaf from the thunder.

We pulled, we hauled and we shifted, zigging and zagging to keep the wind to our advantage. If the British caught us in their glasses, they must have thought they beheld our beauteous frigate in a devil-dance and, if at all superstitious, bore away.

We sailed triumphantly into Corunna where we were well received, although what we were doing there none would say. Certainly, it proved not the best stop for keeping the people in order. The reaction of the insubordinate to the let down of tensions was both fierce and wild, and they jumped ship, although most returned.

The *Alliance* needed repairing even yet, and who were called upon to accomplish this but me and my underlings. There was no shore leave for us, an order we at first resented, but afterward, when we saw what happened to the others who disobeyed, we agreed it was for the best.

Those of the crew who went on land disgraced us shamefully with their wild and destructive acts, but they paid dearly. They lay sick for days with dysentery and vomiting from unclean food and drink. Several contracted pox and lay rolling in agony while the ship's doctor refused to go near them. He finally sent laudanum down to ease the pain and ordered them to cauterize one another with live flame. I did my part to bring us safe to Corunna—that I did—and still no friendly word, let alone a word of praise from Commodore Jones.

Well, now, I have sent my letter of resignation, and be sure he will not deny it. May my path be soon a homeward one, for I long for my own town of Newbury, Massachusetts, and my own family.

I long for the sights of home, the sound of my mother's voice, and the arms of my own, raven haired Sarah Orcutt. I would see the face of my beloved son, now grown four years old and a stranger to me. I thank God, now, for those brave captains who have brought us the letters from home and returned ours to you.

Henry Lunt's letter home revealed his melancholia and that his relationship with John Paul Jones had deteriorated. He wrote:

> I can stand this condition no longer, which is the Commodore's practice of blaming me for everything. Feeling he wishes to be rid of me, I have sat me down and wrote my resignation, begging leave to return to America on the first possible instance.

Henry wrote his letter of resignation, and it is a matter of record as follows:

> Sir, you have treated me with disrespect all the late cruze, which makes my life very unhappy when I think of it, and that almost all of the time. I have often said, and I say it still, I would sooner go on a warlike ship with Captain Jones than any man ever I saw—if I could be treated with respect.

Lunt dispatched a boy with the letter, and at once he felt at peace. He had acquainted the Commodore with his discontent, but he did not expect a favorable reaction. It was against all the rules, as outlined by Jones, for one of lesser rank to complain to a higher officer.

Lunt made preparations for leaving ship, putting his few belongings together. As he did so, much of the immediate past must have flashed through his mind. There was much to remember. Lunt had begun with Jones on the *Alfred*, and moved with him to the gun deck of the *Providence*, one of a few chosen by Jones. Their service together had, up to then, been on five ships of war, each coming through with hardly a scratch. It seemed that service must now come to an end.

## 20

## BACK TO L'ORIENT

It has been written of John Paul Jones over and over again that he was possessed of all social graces and had a magnetic personality with great powers of persuasion. His reaction to Henry Lunt's letter of resignation was one softly sentimental and typical of the commodore. Whatever melancholic spirit had governed the harassment of his second lieutenant, it now took flight and was replaced by one of fawning contrition.

Jones was sick and lying in his bunk when Lunt's letter reached him. He reeled to his feet and ordered his aide to dress him. He raised his voice—for once in a roar—calling for Richard Dale. The first lieutenant came running, registering consternation at this unusual performance. Jones pushed Lunt's letter at him.

Pacing the cabin, the commodore clenched his hands together. It might have been that he never knew until then what he had been doing to a long-time ship mate; one whose esteem he valued, whose prowess he admired, and whose presence he needed.

Dale helped to calm the commodore, and he reassured him that the situation was not irredeemable. He knew both these men and understood the chasms that widened between them because of the differences in their origins. He also knew the similarities that bound them together. Richard Dale was the perfect prototype of the stiff and disciplined officer of the future. He, of all the young lieutenants, most fitted specifications laid down by Jones when he wrote to Joseph Hewes: "A Commander in the Navy ought to be a man of strong, well-connected sense, with a tolerable education; a gentleman as well as a seaman, both in theory and practice.

If Jones was inclined to hold Dale up as an example, it was

because he wanted all of his officers to arrive at the same degree of perfection as the lieutenant from Virginia. It is to Dale's credit that his contemporaries regarded him with liking and respect in spite of the commodore's constant display of favoritism.

Henry Lunt, who ever after received all praise and credit from Jones, never quite understood his own position. He looked physically too much like the commodore, and he acted too much like him for complete accord, for no man can tolerate constantly his mirrored self.

Dale, standing off from the two, saw the situation for what it was. He saw the role of Lunt in all of its aspects. Jones might call upon his second lieutenant for formal duty one moment, and at the next moment use him as a stand-in when secret meetings called him away. The ambivalence of their relationship was a strain on both.

When Jones saw Lunt as his alter ego, he expected the same flawless judgments, the same fanatical drive as his own. Actually, he was no harder on Henry Lunt than he was on John Paul Jones.

The commodore was certain to have been dismayed, if not altogether surprised, that Henry Lunt would even consider leaving him after all they had been through. He resolved at once that this should, and would not, happen. Nor did it. Jones was really sick, but he had Richard Dale accompany him while he sought out his second lieutenant. Here again he revealed the greatness of his spirit in not having ordered his subordinate to come to him.

He took Lunt to one side. Whatever passed between them then has not been clearly stated. Lunt, in a second reaction of regret, probably was not hard to win over. The entire affair and its outcome certainly did more to improve morale at a time when it was most needed. A renewed spirit among officers of the *Alliance* extended, at least temporarily, to the people. They might even have made the trip to America without the unpleasantness that followed had they not, for one last and final time, met up with Captain Pierre Landais.

John Paul Jones made Henry Lunt a promise that when their term of service together officially ended, and they were to part company, he would write an appropriate answer to that letter of resignation, one that Lunt could cherish and exhibit with pride for the rest of his life. The Commodore did not forget to keep that promise.

The *Alliance* sailed from Corunna on January 28, 1780, and, after an unsuccessful cruise of about two weeks, she entered the outer harbor at L'Orient about mid February. Jones was thin and exhausted. His eyes were inflamed and sore. He left the *Alliance* in the road at Groix, trusting Richard Dale and Henry Lunt to move the frigate up to L'Orient. Jones went directly to the home of a friend for rest and recuperation.

There was something wrong with the *Alliance*. She had outstripped the British and saved their lives, but she had been so unruly all during the recent voyage, her sailing so defective, they dared not cruise her further. The two lieutenants went below to determine what was interfering with rudder responses. They soon discovered what was awry. By order of eccentric Captain Landais, her ballast had been stretched along her transoms from stern to stern. Lieutenant Dale and Lunt had a hearty laugh at Landais's expense over this, and Jones, when informed, was moved to wittily remark, "There is one idea Landais can claim as his own."

When they had altered the odd arrangement of ballast, they found this was only one of many items, below and above, needing attention.

Meanwhile his enemies in France continued to harass the commodore. They attempted to place significance, detrimental to their king, on the *Alliance*'s visit to Spain.

Much of their slander, Lafayette and Franklin were able to put down. But when John Paul Jones was accused of a strong dislike of Frenchmen, he himself made answer. He replied, "As an American officer and as a man, I affectionately love and respect the Character and Nation of France. I hope the alliance with France will last forever."

The American crew was discouraged and homesick. Before long, Jones had for them what he hoped was good news. The *Alliance* had been ordered home, and they were to carry as ballast some important goods: 150 stand of arms which Franklin had obtained from M. Sartine, French minister of marine, and bales of material to make uniforms for George Washington's ragged and freezing army at Valley Forge.

The *Alliance* had to be repaired at once. Jones sent Franklin a long list of materials needed for this purpose. The commodore assumed the French government would foot the bill, but the French coffers were very low due to the profligate spending of the last two ruling monarchs. Franklin wrote in return that strict frugality had to be observed in repairs to the *Alliance*, for Franklin himself would be the one to pay.

Jones, as was his custom, directed the workmen as they performed with their accustomed skill. While he was busy with this, Landais initiated his first move to regain command of the *Alliance*. He also asked for the return of his trunks. His approach made Franklin uneasy, and the good doctor made Landais a sharp reply. He wrote in a letter dated March 12, 1780, saying:

> I think you so imprudent, so litigious and quarrelsome a man, even among your best friends, that peace and good order and, consequently, the quiet, regular subordination so necessary to success are, where you preside, impossible. . . .
>
> Your military operations I leave to more capable judges. If, therefore, I had twenty ships of war, I would not give one of them to Captain Landais. The same temper that excluded him from the French Marine would weigh equally with me.

Franklin agreed, however, that Landais could claim his belongings from the *Alliance*, and arranged passage home for him on the American merchant ship *Luserne*. The doctor warned that Landais, if he went to America, must understand that once there, he would have to stand before a court-martial to answer to the charges preferred for his performance in the *Bon Homme Richard-Serapis* battle.

Allowing Landais anywhere near the *Alliance* was the first bad move. The second was acceptance by Jones of four passengers for America. One of these men was Arthur Lee, who, with Samuel Adams, had sponsored Landais in the first place. There was every indication of conspiracy in the arrival of all these men at once.

As they worked to repair the *Alliance*, the men talked among themselves, and it was soon apparent to those most loyal that there was skulduggery afoot. Legitimate complaints were being seized upon and swelled all out of proportion. Most effective was the rapidly growing discontent over money owed the crew. The sailors had received not one cent of wages, nor any of the prize money due them. Many were destitute, having lost all when the *Bon Homme Richard* went down.

The people had grumbled before. This was expected of men long away from home and shut up in close quarters together. The area of pocketbook is one prodigiously sacred to all wage-earners. But the sudden surgence of disagreeable protest that burst like a bomb all around was too fast for those in top command to catch. In vain did they point out that a return to America was close at hand, and there, such matters would be dealt with faster. In vain did they suggest that it would be very impractical for the seamen to change their allegiance at such a late hour.

By mid April with the *Alliance* repaired, loaded, and ready to sail, discontent among crew members was so apparent, Jones felt the smart move would be to get up and go on the first fair wind. When he realized he would have mutiny on his hands if he tried to go home without advancing some wages, he was forced into another move.

When the *Alliance* had arrived at L'Orient from Corunna, the first ship they saw was the *Serapis*, lying at anchor there. Lieutenant Richard Dale sent word to Jones, still convalescing from his illness.

The commodore returned from leave earlier than he should have, feeling and looking much better but still weak. He lost no time in setting wheels in motion to have the *Serapis* made the permanent property of the American government. Here was a ship his people had earned with blood—they were entitled to it; he was determined they should have it. Jones obtained the signatures of all his men under his own.

The French had other ideas about the warship captured from the British, and they intended to make book on it. Therefore, another hope of the Americans on France's side of the water was dashed. Not only did the French refuse to give up the *Serapis*, M. Sartine sent French officers to take possession of that ship and the *Countess of Scarborough* as well.

Discouraged, but not defeated, Jones knew that he would have to salvage either prize money or wages for his men. At mid April he set out for Paris. His interview there with M. Sartine, anxious to salve the Americans, seemed successful beyond his expectations. Sartine, with Jones before him, issued orders for the immediate sale of other prizes according to American laws and terms of the concordat. Satisfied, Jones returned to L'Orient.

The money promised did not come, and it was soon apparent that M. Sartine had been indulging in the old game of promises, promises, never kept.

Franklin, ever faithful, was able to supply out of his pocket only a drop in the bucket. He sent all that he could spare—2,400 livres—out of which the men received only a pittance apiece, which appeased them not at all.

The commodore began to worry over the security of his own position. His people were beginning to spread doubts among themselves as to congressional backing of Jones's commission. Jones knew, having been informed by both Lafayette and Franklin, that the French court was eager for a sight of him and was losing patience. He finally went to Versailles.

Versailles was more than ready for John Paul Jones. Hailed as a hero wherever he went, subjects thronged the streets to catch sight of this brave and controversial figure. Summoned before the throne of Louis XVI, he was graciously received. Queen Marie Antoinette had him attend her at the opera.

Jones could speak French well, and he had no trouble with communications. For the first time, he could give full vent to his own courtliness and could exercise to the fullest his poetic facility. He wrote many effusive letters complimenting the ladies and gentlemen alike, all of important, noble heritage.

It was a time of excitement and stimulation for John Paul Jones; one of the few he was to enjoy to such an extent in his lifetime. He would have been less than human had he not relaxed for a while to enjoy this extreme and well-deserved adultation. It greatly enhanced the American image beyond the crude and homespun one projected by the British intelligence.

Jones did not forget his men at this time, although some have hinted that he might have. He constantly beseeched Dr. Franklin to use his influence and exhorted M. Sartine to keep his word. He pressed only for what he felt was owed. He boasted, thinking to excite their vanities.

Jones promised that he would return to America with the

beautiful *Alliance* to annex there, with Franklin's aid, a newer and bigger warship—the *America* of seventy-four guns and still on the ways at Portsmouth, New Hampshire. The commodore declared he would then return to France with enough American seamen to man ten or twelve frigates that the French would contribute.

This was thinking big, and King Louis liked such thinking. He and his queen were big spenders. They decided that they would no longer withhold honors that they had planned for John Paul Jones. King Louis XVI invested the commodore with the Cross of Military Merit—an honor never before given to an individual who was not a French subject—and he conferred upon him the title of chevalier.

In addition, the King had M. Sartine write and inform the American Congress that his majesty was ready and willing to approve any of Jones's projects which would be supported by Congress. Jones had played his hand so well that he overplayed it. However the commodore had done great work for American-French diplomatic relations, so great that he himself was ultimately to get lost in the shuffle. But that was still later.

Benjamin Franklin sent a letter to Samuel Huntington, Esq., president of Congress. He called attention to the brave conduct of Commodore Jones who "has done great honor to the American Flagg."

On May 29, Jones dined with M. Sartine, and at that time handed that gentleman a warrant containing wages due his men. The warrant had been co-signed by Benjamin Franklin. For about the twentieth time, Sartine promised payment without delay. Jones had no choice but to accept his word, with the hope that Franklin's signature would turn the trick, all else having failed. He later wished he had camped on Sartine's doorstep until he had the money in hand.

But Jones really could not wait. On June 1, he received word from Dr. Franklin that the *Alliance* must sail at once to aid in the defense of Philadelphia.

The American Congress was being beset on all sides for money and equipment for the army and the navy. It failed to see where one was more important than the other. Congress had yet to receive those promised supplies from France, and the personnel problems that plagued Jones and Franklin were not entirely clear to those who were thousands of miles away on the other side of the ocean. America was, furthermore, tired of having her bravest and most competent naval officer, John Paul Jones, defending the shores of France while American waters were being riled by the British. The capital, Philadelphia, now was threatened.

## 21

## PERSONNEL PROBLEMS

John Paul Jones left the French court with his head in the clouds. Armed with great promises, he firmly believed that he would, in the future, have a fleet of ships provided by France to wage a great naval offensive against England. He was certain that this was the instrument by which America would eventually become a great naval force.

Jones had no doubt that Congress would back his plan. In his idealistic state of mind, the impractical side of his nature was in sway. With incredible naiveté, he accepted the role of hero as if it were a lasting one. He had reached as high as he could go in France, even to the throne of her monarch. He had done all these things in the name of the American flag. His position, he thought, could not be more secure.

The eagle eye of Benjamin Franklin was quick to catch the commodore's mood of over-confidence. While pleased that the dashing Jones had captivated romantic France, he felt moved to issue a warning. Franklin took Jones aside and told him, "There is little of credit to be put in promises made during moments of exhileration." Jones was not in a mood to hear criticism, however, and, in one of his rare slips, he set himself up for further disappointment.

The one problem both Jones and Franklin had left dangling was Captain Landais, who had never stopped working for what he considered his legal rights. They were, therefore, caught off balance when Pierre Landais, well fortified for trouble, projected himself upon the scene at L'Orient while Jones was still away and Henry Lunt was playing his role of stand-in.

Landais's timing was excellent. While claiming his belongings on the *Alliance*, the former captain was quick to notice the sullen faces of the men about him, and some of them even cheered his presence. He made the most of this opportunity. Speaking to underlings as if he regarded them as equals, Landais told them they were victims of a masterful deception to make the commodore and his officers rich. Jones, he told them, was even now at the French court spending their money in wasteful extravagances.

This brought the men up short. They had thought their commodore still on his own bridge, where they had seen him a few minutes before. Henry Lunt and Richard Dale could no longer sustain the deception. They rushed down from the bridge and broke up the rally, but not before Landais had made his telling shot by pointing out the deception of placing Henry Lunt on the bridge to make the men believe that Captain Jones was on his ship. Landais then left, but his departure was only temporary.

Then, Arthur Lee arrived to back Landais's every contention. The Virginian, American commissioner to France, was sincerely opposed to John Paul Jones, but for reasons never made quite clear. There is evidence that he and Samuel Adams, together, formed a prejudice when supporters of Jones protested the commissioning of Landais in the first place. Joseph Hewes and Robert Morris, powerful members of the American Marine Committee, had taken their views from Benjamin Franklin, who had had Landais investigated before he even commanded the *Alliance*. Franklin had intended the *Alliance* for Jones, and his enemies seized upon this as his reason for not wanting Captain Landais.

Adams and Lee insisted that the appointment of a French captain on the *Alliance* would greatly please the Marquis de Lafayette, who sailed on the *Alliance* on her maiden voyage to France. Such thinking was both fallacious and impractical. While the courteous Lafayette could not refuse such a flattering gesture from the American government he so supported, it was he who quietly confided to Franklin that Captain Landais had been maneuvered out of the French navy for the same traits constantly manifested while in the service of America.

Franklin then regretted that he had ever allowed Landais to bring the *Alliance* to France, for whenever the deposed French captain boarded the beautiful frigate, he stuck there like glue and was impossible to remove.

The time would come when Arthur Lee would finally regret he had ever heard of Captain Pierre Landais, let alone traveled aboard ship with him, but that change in attitude came about too late to prevent the chaotic events in between.

Landais, shrewd at all times, capitalized on his advantageous position. He knew without a doubt that he could again captain the *Alliance*—and soon. First, he approached Arthur Lee for a statement supporting his claim to command of the frigate, and Lee was glad to oblige. This statement was then presented to the crew.

There were slightly under 400 sailors on the *Alliance*. Of these, 116 signed the statement to be placed before Dr. Benjamin Franklin. Included was a demand for six months of wages which were owed them and "the return of their rightful Captain Landais."

Franklin was enraged. All of his efforts failed to keep the dissension among the Americans from public domain. What really hurt was the fact that the document presented by Landais had been signed by three officers of the *Alliance*, Captain Parke of the marines, First Lieutenant Degge, and Master Buckley. These three had also signed the original articles drawn against Landais at Texel.

In order to save face with the French court, Franklin could not lightly discard a document signed by Lee as American commissioner to France. He was forced into action; a deplorable position which further enraged him.

Franklin, in his role as ambassador, let it be known that Arthur Lee was en route to America and therefore, in addition to being misguided and misled, was acting without authority. The doctor then entered a complaint against Pierre Landais as a fomenter of mutiny and gave out an order for his arrest.

Events leading up to this final action moved so fast, with Jones first at L'Orient and then at Paris, that it was impossible to tie the situation down.

Lee and Landais, once their document was ready, were spurred to great mutinous acts. Lee stood up before the *Alliance* crew and told the people that only Landais was under direct orders from Congress, which took precedence over orders from Benjamin Franklin. He then supported Landais in the allegation that Jones had been commissioned by Franklin alone.

It must be remembered that many Americans on the *Alliance* came out from Boston with the ship in full knowledge of Landais's appointment. These men had no absolute knowledge as to the status of Jones. Only a handful of men, Lieutenants Dale and Lunt included, had positive knowledge of the captaincy handed Jones by Congress in the spring of 1776.

Jones had more sentiment in his favor than did Landais, at least at the start of the latter's drive for supremacy. Many of the men found it hard to forget the trials and triumphs of their lives these past months under the commodore. Jones had inspired them to acts of bravery. Landais preached only discouragement, degradation, and abject humiliation, unless all should follow him. There was no time for philosophical comparisons between harrassments. Landais arrived back in L'Orient from a hurried and unsuccessful visit to Franklin on April 9. But he had no intention of obeying the doctor's order that he go home on any ship other than the *Alliance*. In two days time, Landais had influenced a large number of the *Alliance* crew. He now urged them to demand an accounting of all prizes and money due them. What Landais failed to tell them was that he was the one who had sent many of their prizes to Norway, where they had been promptly turned over to the British by that government.

When Jones heard what was afoot, he resolved to stay with this issue of prize money until he got some results. He felt that he could regain the confidence of his crew in this fashion, and perhaps he could have. He left for Paris on April 13 and was away six weeks. He knew this was too long, but he dared not go back without the money.

He was again feted and admired to the point of exhaustion, but the vulgar topic of finances was one not allowed in social circles. The lords and ladies of France were not interested in serious topics while Jones, the hero of the hour, was in their midst. He was human enough to enjoy it all, but anxiety finally drove him back to L'Orient—his mission unaccomplished.

From the end of May through June, Benjamin Franklin was

barraged with letters from Lee. These included letters from individual crew members. Following all these came Landais's request for reinstatement as captain of the *Alliance.*

Franklin had previously written his famous letter informing Landais he would never endorse his appointment to any ship. He had a different message for the crew, to whom he paid all respect and honor when he wrote:

> I believe you to be brave men and lovers of your country and its glorious cause. I am persuaded you have been ill advised and misled by the artful and malicious representations of some persons guessed at. Take in good part this friendly counsel from an old man who is your friend.
>
> Go home with your ship. Do your duty faithfully and cheerfully. Behave respectfully to your Commander, and I am persuaded that he will do the same for you. Thus, you will not only be happier in your voyage but you will commend yourselves to the future favors of Congress and your Country.

The above letter was written on June 7. On June 12, Franklin wrote to Jones informing him of action he had taken. The ambassador concluded his letter with this warning: "You are likely to have great trouble. I wish you well through it. You have shown your abilities in fighting. You now have an opportunity to show another necessary part in the character of a great chief—your abilities in policy."

Doctor Franklin had been highly successful in his efforts to gather war supplies for General Washington. What he could not seem to do for the ragged American sailors, he was able to do for the equally ragged soldiers. The purses of many a noble gentleman and lady were opened. Many gave goods. Indeed, so much in materials and ordnance were obtained it soon became apparent that another ship would be needed to convoy everything to America.

Forthcoming, on loan from France, was a fine, copper-bottomed ship named the *Ariel.* Both Franklin and Jones concurred that an early departure of the *Ariel* was necessary. It soon became evident that this could not be accomplished until the matter of the *Alliance* was settled.

Jones boarded the *Alliance* and summoned the people amidship. There he placed them at ease, and he stood as observer while Lieutenant Dale read the commodore's original commission from Congress. He then had Henry Lunt, second lieutenant, read the order from Dr. Franklin giving command of the *Alliance* to Jones.

The reaction of his people right before his eyes brought dismay. The commodore had never contemplated a disorderly demonstration directed against him. In contrast with the many who raised their voices and shook clenched fists, only a few stood militarily at ease. Jones made haste to leave the ship.

The handful of dollars he had distributed among the men had made no obvious difference. Some even threw the money overboard. It amounted to little more than ten dollars apiece. Jones dared not promise the men more money unless positive he could deliver. He went ashore to confer with the French authorities. While he was gone, matters came to a head.

Captain Landais had the advantage. His spies told him what had happened. He immediately perceived that the time had come to make his move. Lieutenant Degge was selected to read to the crew the order from Commissioner Lee that Captain Landais was to take command of the *Alliance* at once. It was carefully emphasized that only under such a command would Congress authorize the payment of wages and prize money due the men. There was never a moment's doubt. A majority decided in favor of Landais. The former captain lost no time in going aboard and taking command.

Survival was now reduced to a choosing up of sides. Lieutenants Dale and Lunt engaged in an immediate nose count. The result was extremely disappointing to them. Only forty-five men were still standing firmly behind their commodore and his officers. This meant that even the *Bon Homme Richard* contingent had split. There was only one course to take. The men for Jones went ashore—in the nick of time it is said, for Landais planned to place them all in irons.

The mad captain then unloaded some of his cargo—so important to the war effort at home—in order to make room for a hug and elaborate coach that Arthur Lee was determined to take back to America. Jones had previously refused to make room for this same coach.

The commodore, advised by messenger that his loyal crew members were now beached, threw himself on a horse and galloped posthaste back to L'Orient. Seeing at once the hopelessness of the situation, Jones ordered his beached and pitifully small crew to load the supplies on the *Ariel* as best they could, but her holds were already full. Giving orders to the French garrison at Port Louis to block the harbor, Jones returned to Versailles with fire in his eyes. He went straight to Benjamin Franklin.

Before leaving, Jones had given orders for Landais's arrest, but the French refused to honor this until given the go ahead by their own commissioner. When M. Sartine heard of this, he gladly endorsed that order, but Jones did not know this until his return to L'Orient. By that time things were popping in earnest.

Landais, under Lee's encouragement, had the *Alliance* warped and towed out of the inner roads of Groix into the narrow strait directly in line with Port Louis. The guns of the fort were aimed dead on him, and there his luck began to run out. He discovered that the French authorities had had a barrier drawn across the channel to prevent his departure. Then, his men began to lose faith in him.

Landais had Lee stand with him on the quarter deck of the *Alliance* while he, his voice raised to a paranoic shriek, promised all sorts of wild and impossible promises to the gaunt, battle-worn, ragged, and, now, uneasy crew that stood beneath him.

For the people, this was the beginning of total disillusionment, and during the long days and weeks that followed, homesickness spread until it had become a disease of epidemic force. They were feeling less and less like heroes and more and more like the victims of a hoax.

Summoned posthaste by Lieutenant Dale in person, Jones reappeared on the scene. Now the commodore had the upper hand. M. de Thevenard, French officer of the fort, had presented to Captain Landais the positive orders of Dr. Franklin that men and the ship, *Alliance*, were to be surrendered to Commodore Jones.

Captain Landais refused to surrender.

M. de Thevenard awaited the pleasure of Commodore Jones.

One or two broadsides from the fort would easily sink the *Alliance*. The gunners were ready to go into action.

The situation was stalemate, but it was a time when the two contenders, Jones and Landais, stood starkly revealed, each for the exact type of individual he was. None, not even the deserters of the *Alliance* would ever again waver in their loyalty and alliance to their commodore.

John Paul Jones backed down. Even some of his most vicious critics later defended his decision. The *Alliance* was freighted with stores of great value to General Washington, whose men were impoverished as to materials for survival, let alone to make war. Furthermore, a sizeable minority of seamen left on the *Alliance*, either through kinship or association, were related to those who had left her. These men now wanted out. They vainly sought liberation from the situation in which they now found themselves. Would Jones, the disciplinarian have given the order for the destruction of an American ship? He would indeed, once convinced this was the right thing to do.

Daily, during the long confrontation, the sadistic Captain Landais lined up on the deck of the *Alliance* men who had served on the *Bon Homme Richard*, in order that Jones could look down the long cannons of Fort Louis upon the men who had so valiantly served with him.

Captain Parke and Lieutenant Degge, on the *Alliance*, protested this action and, for the first time, came up against a Captain Landais with bared teeth. He drew his sword and pressed its flat side against the stomach of Captain Parke.

For more than a month, this situation prevailed. Each day, more seamen on the *Alliance* were placed in irons. Said one historian, John Abbott, "Bitter was the correspondence that flew during the six weeks the *Alliance* lay trapped, riding silently and beautifully, her guns ready for action but impervious to the tumult raging about and concerning her."

Daily, Commodore Jones was confronted by the anguished faces of the gaunt and worn-out members of his loyal contingent. Sick of poverty, sick of war, and sick of situations that found Americans fighting Americans, they had thoughts for one thing only—home and the arms of loved ones too long in separation from them. The British, who had contended with these defiant and undefeatable Americans, both in prison and at sea, would have felt well rewarded could they but have seen them at that time.

Jones refused to yield openly to sentiment. Instead, he chafed and harped on duty. He fretted that the goods in the *Alliance* would not be delivered on time. When he had himself sufficiently convinced, the gallant commodore gave the order for the barrier to be lifted. The noble nature of Jones could not permit the destruction of an American ship. A letter from Jones to Franklin, dated at L'Orient on June 21, confirms this. Jones wrote: "Your humanity will I know justify the part I acted in preventing a scene that would have rendered me miserable for the rest of my life."

The *Alliance* sailed for home with the regretting, and now eternally loyal, seamen of the *Bon Homme Richard* confined below her decks. With the *Alliance*, at Jones's insistence, went several American vessels which had been waiting all this time for convoy. Jones was now left alone with only forty-five men of the *Bon Homme Richard*, including his own faithful lieutenants, Richard Dale and Henry Lunt. Many new faces would have to be added before he could sail the *Ariel* home to America. This was a situation the commodore could always handle.

With his decision to release the *Alliance* came a kind of peace, and once she had gone, tensions were greatly released. John Paul Jones was able to react both graciously and appreciatively when evidence of the French court's high esteem for him was shown at a time when he particularly needed encouragement. All forty-five of the *Ariel*'s present complement, officers and men alike, joined in toasting their commodore's French promotion to the title of chevalier conferred by King Louis XVI. With his diploma came a beautiful gold-hilted sword.

From that time on, Jones was never to refer to himself again as commodore, a title that had come to mean to him little more than mockery due to malicious Captain Landais and his supporters.

John Paul Jones, from then on, was chevalier to his loyal and ever faithful forty-five. Never would they put into words the hurt they knew existed in his sensitive heart when the title which would have been so welcome from the America he loved was bestowed on Jones by a foreign government.

## 22

## THE COURT-MARTIAL

The *Alliance* was on an unbelievable voyage. This proud frigate, deserving the best in seamanship, suffered the worst possible. Captain Landais, without a doubt mentally unbalanced, performed like the caricature of a naval officer. Before they were a day at sea, he had most of his supporters wishing they were safe on dry land, on which side of the ocean mattered not.

Captain Parke of the marines was placed in irons as soon as they were at sea. Shrieking that this was in payment for Parke's protestations when the crewmen of the late *Bon Homme Richard* were lined up before the cannons of Fort Louis, Landais promised similar or worse treatment for all those who questioned his authority.

Lieutenant Degge, before he could open his mouth one way or the other, was the next target. He, too, was placed in irons. Master Buckley, shaking in his shoes, was elevated in rank, a dubious honor he could have done without.

Captain Landais then played at seamanship like a child abusing a toy boat. The crew nearly went out of their minds as watches were split until no man knew for sure who was expected up or down. Landais ordered the sails down in a fresh breeze and up in a calm. Ships sailing with him in convoy were soon lost to sight. Some were taken as prizes once out of the protection of the *Alliance*. Watching his fleet scatter, Landais chortled with glee. Pretending he was after the merchant ships to bring them back, he ordered the *Alliance* off course. He wasted days tacking back and forth across the North Atlantic.

The officers of the ship were worn out. They conspired with Arthur Lee, and, together, they confronted Captain Landais. They assured him he was jeopardizing the ship and its precious cargo by his antics. They threatened that they would surrender if they were attacked. For once, the mad captain yielded, and, under Lee's insistence, he allowed the *Alliance* to return to course, there to proceed steady on.

Arthur Lee had defied Captain Landais, and for days the captain brooded. Then he turned on his former champion. One day at table, Lee reached for a first helping of meat. Landais seized a long knife and brandished it at his sponsor. The Virginian was forced to retire in fear of his life. He dared not draw his sword, for Landais had proved himself a most proficient swordsman against poor Captain Cottineau of the *Pallas*. Word of this had gotten around.

The voyage took so long, food supplies began to run out. Buckley, noting that they were now off the Grand Banks of Newfoundland, ordered the men to fish. Landais rescinded the order and threatened to kill any person caught eating fish.

Then, Lee received his just desserts. Hearing a great commotion on deck, he rushed forward to see what was happening. He arrived just in time to see his massive and beautiful ceremonial coach pitched over the side. The *Alliance* rocked under the lightened load and back swell of the sea. The former commissioner had had enough. He gathered the officers together and told them they must inform the crew that Captain Landais was suffering a nervous breakdown. He then led them below where Captain Parke, Lieutenant Degge, and the seamen in irons were released.

It is too bad John Paul Jones could not have been present on August 10, after a month and two days at sea, when Landais was forced to give over command of the *Alliance* to Lieutenant Degge. Officers and passengers demanded this in writing. Landais took to his cabin and was confined there under guard.

Degge brought the *Alliance* into the harbor at Boston, Massachusetts, on August 19, 1780, after a voyage of nearly six weeks, and immediately reported his captain insane.

Landais, from his cabin on the *Alliance*, defied all by refusing to come out. He wrote many disjointed letters. An example of this is one to the Navy Board in which he closed saying:

Never before was such things seen and heard of and I conjecture their first step when on shore will be altogether to give me a bad character. Before God! Bring to light the truth. Till then I leave it to your sagacity.

Mr. Degge ordered but to obey him. Then I was surrounded by all the passengers. You will find them out there are very cunning ones among them.

On receipt of this and other letters, the Navy Board ordered Lieutenant Degge to relinquish command to Captain John Barry and to proceed at once to the board's Boston office.

Captain Parke was sent to inform Landais and to escort him off the *Alliance*. The former captain refused to open the door to his quarters. They finally had to break down the door, and it took three men to drag the screaming Captain Landais off the ship.

The Navy Board ordered that the court-martial be held, beginning on the twentieth of November, aboard the *Alliance* in Boston Harbor.

Pierre Landais appeared during his court-martial with all the aplomb of a candidate for a high award, arrogantly self-assured and immaculately attired. He might once again have won many of the uninitiated to his side had the military court moved swiftly. As it turned out, considering all evidence against him, the court proved most lenient.

Captain John Barry, Esq., the presiding officer, was not a man to be hurried through so serious a matter, and it was his determination that a thorough investigation be made into all facts of the case.

The court-martial was assembled on board the *Alliance* in Boston Harbor on the twentieth day of November, 1780, "pursuant to a warrant from the Honourable Navy Board, Eastern Department, directed to John Barry, Esq., Captain and Commander in the Navy of the United States."

If any are given to wonder why the trial was so delayed and finally held without the presence of some of the most important witnesses for the prosecution, there is a very simple answer.

The delay was at the written request of Benjamin Franklin, who, for once, was very disturbed and provoked at John Paul Jones. Rather than being pleased that the commodore had permitted Landais to make off with the *Alliance*, he was angry.

Franklin was resolved that Jones and his junior officers would be present at Landais's court-martial in America, if it was at all possible.

As for John Paul Jones, he was hurt by Franklin's attitude and understandably frantic in his efforts to get back home—at last to engage in a face-to-face confrontation that he was sure would rid them of Landais for good.

The very elements conspired to further frustrate those in France and lend assistance to their tormentor. The *Ariel*, with Jones in command, sailed on October 8, and was hardly under way when she was caught in a ferocious storm which raked the shores of France, causing considerable damage.

The chevalier was never closer to foundering in all of his years at sea. The *Ariel* was so badly damaged, they had all they could do to limp her back to L'Orient. What was worse, she could not be readied again under six weeks at the earliest.

On the heels of this bad luck came a message from America to Franklin that Captain Landais had been his old busy self, pleading self-pity and working up a new set of followers. He had lost his old set of champions for good, but Boston had its share of ambitious, self-seeking men who were very happy to listen to Landais's version of what had happened. These opportunists were ready to jump either way once the outcome of the American Revolution was determined. In the meantime, they conspired and pretended to agree with the last person they met. Captain Landis, both an articulate and convincing talker, seemed to them, as he had to many before them, a man worth supporting if one wished to reach high places.

Franklin, when informed of Landais's activities, sent word that the court-martial must begin at once. A new warrant was hastily prepared, striking from it charges which had involved Jones, the *Bon Homme Richard*, and the many acts of insubordination. This had to be done because there was no live testimony to back the accusatory document.

This was another break for Captain Landais. Although there was sufficient evidence of mutiny in the recent altercations aboard the *Alliance*, Landais could plead battle fatigue as reason for his erratic actions and, with proper finesse, turn the charge of mutiny back on his officers and men.

The court-martial was continued by several adjournments to the sixth day of January, 1781 "to inquire into the conduct of Peter Landais, Esq." The records show that Thomas A. Dawes, Jr., was Judge Advocate. Others sitting on the court-martial were as follows: John Barry, Esq., president; Captain Hoystead Hacker, Esq.; Samuel Nicholson, Esq., Lieutenant Silas Devot, Lieutenant Patrick Fletcher, Lieutenant Nicholas Gardner, and of the marines, Lieutenant Samuel Pritchard.

Captain Landais was, as has been said, incredible. Only the snail's pace established by Captain Barry helped to reveal the accused's other nature. Landais was unable to sustain a benign attitude for long and by January was indulging in paranoic outbursts.

If Benjamin Franklin did conspire to delay the trial's end, as some have contended, it is also true that Captain Barry seems to have been one to subscribe to "giving a man enough rope." From Landais's first outburst, Barry was resolved to study him further as he reacted under pressure. Landais, unable to otherwise contain himself, readily obliged.

The accused captain indulged in ridiculous pantomime and much chest thumping. One observer later described it as "beating himself with his fist to black and blue and nigh unto death." Landais, over his legal defender's advice, admitted to all accusations but insisted he was the victim of a "great conspiracy." He placed all of the blame on Arthur Lee, much to Lee's embarrassment, saying all orders, from beginning to end, came from Lee. Landais was able to produce letters written by Lee to this effect which proved damaging to the latter.

The court, having collected all the admissable evidence in its power touching the conduct of Peter Landais, Esq., commander of the *Alliance* during her voyage from L'Orient to Boston, immediately previous to her sailing, and since her arrival at Boston, rendered a decision and were of the unanimous opinion:

> That said Peter Landais, Esq., is guilty of a breach of orders of Congress, and of the orders of the Honble Navy Board Eastern Department dated Boston, December, 1779.

But that said Peter Landais, Esq., in coming away without leave, as afore said, took the advice of the Honble Arthur Lee, Esq., a gentleman learn'd in the Laws and High in Office, and so far is entitled to favor:

Which advice, together with the motives that urged it, will appear by copies of certain letters from said Honble Arthur Lee, Esq., and transmitted herewith.

Secondly, that said Peter Landais is guilty of a further breach of the orders of Congress and of said Navy Board in suffering certain private goods to be brot' in said ship from France and by that means creating an interest on board said ship repugnant to the public service.

Thirdly, that said Peter Landais is guilty of a breach of the first and thirty-seventh articles in the rules for the regulation of the Navy of the United States in not exerting his utmost abilities to inspect the behavior of the passengers, of his officers and crew, and to detect and bring to punishment offenders on board, and in not setting an example to his officers in discharging their duties.

Fourthly, that said Peter Landais is guilty of a breach of the orders of said Navy Board, in not delivering up the ship *Alliance*, her cabin and cabin furniture when said Board ordered him to deliver them up:

But said court, taking into consideration the peculiar circumstances of Capt. Landais, that he was then without credit or money in this country, that he had no comfortable resort but to said ship, recommend said Landais to indulgence.

Said Court conceiving it to be their duty to do so, beg leave further to report that Capt. Landais has, nevertheless greatly suffered from a mutinous disposition in both passengers and officers and from a real mutiny in crew of said ship.

## The Sentence

The Court Martial adjudges the said Peter Landais, Esq., to be broke and rendered incapable of serving in the American Navy for the future.

[Signed]

| | John Barry Prest |
|---|---|
| After which the Court was dissolved | |
| | J. Dawes, J. A. |

Pierre de Landais had a fine heritage. He was born in the year 1731, the youngest son in one of the oldest and proudest families of Normandy. By the time Pierre's generation came along, there was no family fortune, but his aristocratic origins were such that lustre was still connected to his name.

Because of this, the future American naval captain was able to obtain an appointment to a good French naval academy. There he received an excellent indoctrination into navigation and the geometrics of the sea. He was able to graduate with better than passing marks, but he was not able to secure himself a commission. He, therefore, remained a midshipman until he was in his early thirties, when he rose at last to the rank of sub-lieutenant.

Landais blamed his inability to rise in rank to jealousies of schoolmates and the impoverishment of family that could buy no favors at the French admiralty. It was not the story he first told to his sponsors in the American Revolution, but the one he later told when his lies and misrepresentations were found out.

Some say he was drummed out of the French navy when he disclosed some of the maniacal characteristics which later forced him out of the American navy; some say he left out of pique when, in his mid-forties, he still had no commission worth the having.

In 1777, he talked Silas Deane, one of the original three on the American Marine Committee and then commissioner to France, into sending him to America in command of a merchant ship laden with public stores. More important to him, he carried a letter of introduction to Congress, together with a recommendation for a commission in the United States Navy.

Samuel Adams, one of the first Massachusetts men sent to a Continental Congress, was much impressed by Landais, so much so that he was able to influence the Great and General Court of Massachusetts into making Landais an honorary citizen of that state.

Arthur Lee and Samuel Adams headed the group of Landais supporters responsible for his appointment as captain of the frigate *Alliance*, then in the building at Salisbury Point, Massachusetts.

Landais hastened to New England to oversee the outfitting of his new ship. Conservative natives of the area might have been swayed to a mood of tribute to the Marquis de Lafayette, who was venerated by most, but they saw no reason for a hysterical demonstration, and they were not convinced that they should give the command of their beautiful new frigate to a foreigner.

The doubters were supported by another Adams who did not happen to agree with Samuel. John Adams, not impressed with Landais at all, is said to have traveled across the ocean in the *Alliance* as part of an escort for Lafayette. Adams declared in his diary that Landais was jealous of everybody and everything. He had "silence, reserve and a forbidding manner, an inactivity and indecisiveness which would ruin him." John Adams was correct as far as he went. He apparently never caught Landais in one of his attacks of paranoia.

Captain Landais represented himself to the Marine Committee as one highly venerated in the French Royal Navy, and one who had commanded a ship of the line. He boasted that he had been offered and, out of diffidence, refused the Cross of St. Louis.

Those who sponsored Landais believed him without challenge because they wanted to. It happened to fit so nicely into their plans to rid themselves of John Paul Jones and compliment the French government in one fell swoop. They then succeeded in obtaining a commission for Landais and, as has been stated, gave him the command of the beautiful *Alliance.* The maiden voyage across the Atlantic Ocean to L'Orient, the near mutiny on the way, and subsequent events have all been related.

It is quite ironic to realize that, after all was cut and dried, the only person who believed that Landais really wished to justify his American commission was John Paul Jones. Jones, who never could have risen in the Royal Navy of Britain because he was a gardener's son, understood the drive and desire for recognition.

Landais, born to an illustrious family, would never have admitted to such an identification with Jones. Landais never had a decent word for Jones and would fly into a rage at the mere mention of his name.

To the end of his days, Captain Landais hailed himself as the winner of the *Bon Homme Richard-Serapis* Battle. Known as just plain Pierre Landais after his court-martial had broken him, the former captain was never heard to admit that he had lost his commission. After a time, he even gave himself a promotion. He was a pathetic figure moving about New York City, where he chose to live. On July Fourth celebrations each year, and on occasions celebrating the evacuation of New York by the British, he appeared in public in full naval regalia, wearing the American cockade in his hat. He was always neat in appearance until the last.

He finally promoted himself to the rank of admiral and graduated into the uniform of the Continental navy. No one bothered him. No one challenged him. He found fewer and fewer listeners as the years went on. When some who pitied him offered him presents, he haughtily refused them.

Pierre Landais lived to be eighty-seven years of age, and when he died, he received far better consideration than did John Paul Jones, whose grave was lost for years. Landais died in the summer of 1818, and he was buried in the churchyard of St. Patrick's Cathedral. A stone marks his resting place, engraved in his native language as follows:

A le Memoire
de
Pierre de Landais
Ancien Contre-Admiral
au service
Des États-Unis
Qui Disparut
Juin 1818
Age 87 Years

## 23

## HOME ON THE *ARIEL*

After the *Alliance* sailed, the situation among those left behind was nothing less than chaotic. Henry Lunt, who had spent long hours strutting in plain view of the *Alliance* on the ramparts of Fort Port Louis, was both weary and depressed.

It had long been the practice of John Paul Jones to use Lunt as his double, placing the Newbury man on the bridge dressed in one of Jones's fine uniforms, while the commodore was off on one of his junkets to Versailles. This was not done in the spirit of play, but in fine deception to give the men the confidence that their invincible captain was always with them.

Always before, Henry Lunt had enjoyed these moments when he became "the captain," and his sensitive nature was restored as he imitated the great leader's stride and mannerisms. He had not enjoyed looking down the guns of Fort Port Louis into the faces of his compatriots.

While Jones labored desperately to maneuver himself back into Benjamin Franklin's good graces, Lunt stayed on shore with a French family which had befriended him.

There were 500 tons of goods for America still at L'Orient. This did not include those put ashore from the *Alliance* to make room for Arthur Lee's huge coach. There was room on the *Ariel* for only 100 tons more.

Jones, with tongue in cheek, suggested to Dr. Franklin that he ask for the loan of the *Serapis.* Franklin would ask for nothing of the sort. He felt a thorough humiliation and loss of face over the affair of the *Alliance.* For once, he lashed out at Jones as he told him he would regret having yielded to Captain Landais. Jones, in return, gently admonished Franklin by suggesting that Landais would have been out of their hair had they held his court-martial at once in Holland or, at the latest in France.

Lieutenants Richard Dale and Henry Lunt remained, as always, firmly behind their commodore. If Lunt resented, by comparison, the compassion shown the insubordinate seamen of the *Alliance* as opposed to the treatment he had received, he gave no sign. Perhaps, by now, the stoical side of his New England nature had asserted itself, and he better understood Jones.

In July, Jones and his augmented crew went aboard the *Ariel*. There was much to do before they could sail, for the ship was not yet armed. Tardily, the French government came through (Franklin no doubt relented and influenced their decision) and ordered her to be fully equipped as a ship-of-war. Twenty guns were mounted.

With the loyal forty-five to set the pace, the crew loaded the *Ariel* until she was groaning under her ballast. The rest of the public stores for America were then distributed among other American ships at L'Orient waiting for convoy.

It was July in the year 1780 when they went aboard the *Ariel*. It was December before they actually got under way for home, and this was due in part to the ferocious storm, mentioned earlier, that drove them back to port on their first try for home.

They left L'Orient on October 8, on a fair wind with the apparent promise of good weather, but somebody proved not to be an adequate weather prophet. On midnight of October 9, after one day out, the storm came up, and they were caught in it. Almost at once, they were nearly wrecked on the rocks of Penmarque between L'Orient and Brest. The lower yardarms were plunged time and again into the sea, until it became necessary to cut away the foremast.

This was a situation Henry Lunt and the tough, New England sailors were familiar with. They had handled roaring northeastern gales many times before. This one was different, however, and the *Ariel* was in real trouble. Her main mast had gotten out of step and was reeling to and fro, and it seemed that it must either break off below the gun deck or crash through the bottom of the ship. Jones then gave the order for it to be cut away.

Before this could be accomplished, the chain plates parted. The main mast did break off at the gun deck, and it crashed. In coming down, it took with it the mizzenmast and the quarter gallery.

The *Ariel* could do nothing then but roll like a log, and it took all of their efforts to hold on. Men on all sides were calling out to the Almighty, and most felt this to be the inglorious end.

Suddenly, like the answer to prayer, they floated to the windward of the dreaded rock ledge of Penmarque, which this time proved a haven. There, they held on tightly while the storm raged for two days and two nights, causing ship wrecks all about and a considerable loss of lives. Even the deep harbor at L'Orient was wracked, and ships were tossed like paper boats with many overturned completely.

It was like the wrath of God. When the storm was over, the men on the *Ariel* were actually surprised to find themselves still alive and, in the manner of custom, knelt and gave thanks for their deliverance. Then, in practical action, they rigged jury masts and took the *Ariel* limping back to L'Orient. There, certain new members of the crew began to grumble. Some of the loyal forty-five were dour even though they remained silent.

A few of the more ignorant sailors, forever superstitious, began to believe some of the rumors they had late been hearing and wondered if John Paul Jones was not, after all, a demon incarnate or, at the least, a jinx. For the forty-five of the original crew members, it always came back to money. They pressed again for the prize money and wages owed them.

John Paul Jones was distressed that his men had not been paid, and he had done all that he could to get for them what was, he felt, justly due them. For once, he neither blamed nor chastized but, instead, renewed his vow that he would somehow get their money for them; if not on that side of the water, then back home in America.

All Jones wanted now was to fulfill his trust and carry out his recent orders—get the *Ariel* back home with her much needed stores for the American army. Some of the ships he had had in convoy had not weathered the terrible storm, another cause for despondency.

As for his recent fracas with Captain Landais, he no longer made mention of the man or his court-martial. He no longer seemed to care one way or the other. It was as if the ferocious storm had cleansed him of all bitterness.

"For God's sake, go home!" Dr. Benjamin Franklin said, exhausted with John Paul Jones and his problems. He was beyond all reason.

John Paul Jones walked silently, thin and pale. His eyes were green agates set in dark sockets, and he confided to Lieutenant Dale that too many ghosts walked with him. Ghosts also walked with others.

Lieutenant Henry Lunt thought often of his kinsmen and his ultimate separation from them. He thought most of his cousin, Cutting Lunt, twenty-seven years of age when he shipped aboard the Dalton untried in naval warfare. If he had wanted to forget, Jones would never let him. Whenever riled, the commodore would never fail to mention most bitterly the men and the jolly boat "foolishly lost" off the Irish coast.

Richard Lunt, Cutting's brother, was the luckier, Henry often thought, having served always on the *Alliance* and being ambivalent in his loyalties—"not knowing sometimes which was in the right, Captain 'Landy' or Captain Jones."

When the two Lunts who were left got together, it is certain that they talked of family and compared letters from home. It was from Richard that Henry learned with relief that Cutting had again been released from Old Mill Prison by cartel exchange and was now, from choice, back home.

Everybody wanted to go home.

The crew of the *Ariel* was augmented by sailors from off American merchantmen at L'Orient and a few from off the cartel ships. The ship was repaired and ready. On December 18, 1780, she sailed again from the Port Louis gate. This time she would make it, but the adventures of John Paul Jones and his seasoned Americans were not quite over. They were to have one more ocean crossing and one more meeting with the enemy.

Jones was taking with him important dispatches for the Congress from Franklin and enough cargo to be of extreme importance to General Washington and his freezing army. It was decided that they would travel by the southern route, where, at the end of the trade winds, they could make better time. They would seek no prizes and, indeed, expected to encounter few ships in this little traveled lane of the sea.

After several days, in the latitude of Barbadoes, they met up with a British frigate. They were dismayed but undaunted yet.

The *Ariel*, patched and overloaded with cargo, was in no shape to do battle. The situation called for strategy of a kind Jones could deliver. He first tried to elude the oncoming ship under cover of darkness, but morning revealed it to be closer than ever.

Once again, the New Englanders were forced to compensate in application of their sailing skills and to accept the fact that the *Ariel* had neither the class nor the speed of the *Alliance*.

The chevalier saw that action could not be avoided. Now, there was only one thing to do, and they must sacrifice some of their precious cargo. Jones ordered everything overboard that would interfere with an adequate defense. Then the sails and helm were so managed as to conceal their strength in armaments. They intended, if they could, to appear as a lightly armed merchant ship.

John Paul Jones took the initiative. He opened fire from the quarter deck with his stern chasers as soon as the other frigate came within shot of the *Ariel*. Courtesy now required that the two ships speak one another. However, a light wind kept coming between them, and they were forced to glide along together for many hours. At dusk, the frigates came within hailing distance, and the commanders conversed. Jones was told he was speaking the *Triumph* under Captain Pindar. The Americans, upon coming close, had determined that this was a British warship and had immediately raised a British flag. Jones had observed with much relief that his armaments were of equal strength. Should it come to a fight, they had every confidence for an American victory.

The wily chevalier pompously stamped his deck and blustered at Captain Pindar, pretending that he did not believe the *Triumph* to be a ship of the British navy. He claimed that he, Jones, commanded a British ship harmlessly bent on delivering supplies to His Majesty's forces in America. He ordered Captain Pindar to board the *Ariel* and show his commission. This time Jones over-played his role in so ordering about a captain of the Royal Navy. Captain Pindar in return protested the invitation, and he demanded to know the name of the frigate before him. Having played for time in an even match, both captains were ready.

The two frigates were lying side by side, and each had crew and guns ready—men in the tops ready to sharp-shoot. His bluff had failed, and Jones lost no time in going into action. As they raised the Stars and Stripes with a mighty shout, the gun crews of the *Ariel* fired an all-out broadside into the close British frigate. The *Triumph* immediately returned the blow, and there was a steady bombardment for an estimated ten minutes or more.

It was now dark.

Captain Pindar may have surmised by that time that he was up against the legendary Captain Jones. In any case, the British Captain suddenly struck his colors. The Americans ceased firing at once, and Jones accepted unconditional surrender. He then proceeded in the accepted manner of gentlemanly warfare by first caring for his dead and wounded. The *Ariel* gunners abandoned their positions to help carry the wounded below to ship's surgeon. The Chevalier, as was his custom, directed this action. Suddeny, and too late, he was alerted—but not for further onslaught. The *Triumph* was running away. The British frigate had suffered no damage to her sails or rigging and, taking advantage of this, her captain spread every sail and was off. Gentlemanly warfare be hanged!

This was the last war action John Paul Jones and his veteran fighters would share. Without further incident, the *Ariel* proceeded on her way, and they anchored in the Philadelphia road on February 18, 1781. With tears in every eye, the small band of loyal men, dwindled to under forty, parted company. But first, there was work to do. What remained of General Washington's goods had to be gotten ashore.

No man felt particular disappointment that their welcome home was far from the celebration they so deserved. There were too many missing faces; too much tragedy lay raw and bleeding on their memories. It was bitterly cold on the Delaware River. The thoughts of John Paul Jones, Richard Dale, and Henry Lunt, all three, must have been with that earlier day, seemingly now another life, when they had stood young and invincible before the masts of the *Alfred*. Was it only five years before that they had sailed out in that first American fleet under Commodore

Esek Hopkins? Then the shores of the Delaware had been lined with cheering patriots, the harbor filled with brightly decorated small craft. Only a handful of dignitaries awaited them now at the foot of Philadelphia's Walnut Street.

Henry Lunt followed his chevalier into the barge which had come out to scull them ashore. Looking back upon the *Ariel*, her sails furled, her masts and spars like a skeleton against the cold February sky, he seemed to see the ghosts of the *Alliance* and the *Bon Homme Richard* flying in full sail beyond and out toward the sea. At that moment, he bade farewell to his youth, although he was not yet thirty.

## 24

## HONORS FROM CONGRESS

John Paul Jones had been absent from America only a little more than three years and three months when he arrived in Philadelphia on February 18, 1781. He had left on the *Ranger* and returned on the *Ariel*. No person either in the Continental army or navy had earned more prestige than had he, and he was about to receive the recognition due him.

Congress had passed a resolution acclaiming that:

> The thanks of the United States be given to Captain John Paul Jones for the zeal, prudence and integrity with which he has supported the honor of the American flag; for his bold and successful enterprises to redeem from captivity the citizens of these United States who had fallen under the power of the enemy; and, in general, for good conduct and eminent services by which he had added lustre to his character and to the American arms.

The Board of Admiralty added its support and endorsement to the Congressional declaration. Arthur Lee was more than willing now to add his word of praise.

Franklin and Lafayette wrote to him from France, and John Adams wrote to him from The Hague. General George Washington wrote and praised his heroism and his courage.

This was the high spot in Jones's entire career, and he never was known to ask for more. He was more than willing to share his moment of glory with his valiant officers, and he insisted that their names also be inscribed on the records.

Congress, addressing him as commodore, invited him to appear before that body to answer questions and impart whatever intelligence he could concerning treatment accorded him by the Dutch. This was important, as John Adams was most insistent that sentiment favorable to America in its fight for liberty was on the rise in Holland. Correspondence indicates that Jones, whatever he personally felt after being driven toward the arms of the British fleet in the *Alliance* from Texel, was most carefully considerate of the Dutch officials, and he dwelt more on the assistance they had given in conducting British prisoners back to France to exchange for Americans. John Paul Jones told all, in whatever area he could, concerning his service to his country during his three and one half years away. He was honest in his appraisal of Pierre Landais. He was also very generous, and he even went so far as to say that he felt the former captain was sincere in his devotion to the American cause although "sick in mind."

When Jones had answered all their questions, they were quite satisfied that he had done all that he could to harass the enemy, rescue American prisoners, and bring home stores. They couldn't have asked for more. John Paul Jones then took a well-earned rest, and he engaged in some socializing, a role he was well suited for once he had attended to matters more urgent.

It was never the commodore's custom to make a public appearance without his officers to attend him. Richard Dale and Henry Lunt were most ideal in such a role, and Jones knew that the three made a striking picture when strutting together. They were proud officers of the Continental navy in their buff-colored knee britches and cut-away coats of navy blue with brass buttons; each wore braid scrambled according to his rank. A white shirt with ruffled stock and wristlets lent the purity of youth to each weather-beaten face. Each wore his hair neatly clubbed. Their tricons, with American cockade jauntily set, were seldom on their heads. They were carried, instead, under their arms, where they were more accessible for frequent sweeping bows to the ladies as they moved along.

Richard Dale, the gentleman from Virginia, fell easily into the role of gallant according to the fashion set by the French court that was so popular during the colonial period.

Henry Lunt, on the other hand, had required considerable

coaching, especially at first when they moved under the eyes of the snobbish French aristocrats.

Only under protest did the bucolic New Englander don such finery as was necessary to his dual role when he was set up to impersonate the chevalier. Making a suitable leg was difficult for him, and he could enjoy reducing both Jones and Dale into helpless roars of mirth at his reeling and staggering about.

When Henry Lunt left Philadelphia for home, John Paul Jones was willing to let him go. His scheming mind was already looking ahead to when the largest and most perfect frigate of them all would be his.

The seventy-four gun *America*, which had lain these past six years unfinished on the ways at Langdon's Island, Portsmouth, New Hampshire, had been ordered finished by the Congress. By unanimous vote, Jones was given command, and he immediately started politicking to bring back his officers and able seamen. Still believing completely in his own indestructibility, he saw fulfillment of his dream and his promise that he would gather and bring to France an American fleet of warships unsurpassed by any. In the meantime, a trip home would do the people good.

Anxious as he was to return to home, Henry Lunt found this period of adulation a heady one and all too brief. For the first time, the indignities and travail of the immediate past seemed almost worth the candle. Lunt's cup of happiness was full indeed when he was offered his first commission as a commander in the United States Navy and captain of a ship out of Baltimore, Maryland, running goods of war. To be sure, this was not a fighting ship as he would have wished, but it was enough for Captain Henry Lunt. He was both happy and satisfied. Only one matter remained unsettled. There was still the important detail of the wages and prize money owed John Paul Jones, his officers, and the people. When approached concerning this, Jones promised that he would never stop pressing until each man had his due.

Henry Lunt knew the chevalier to be a man who, to the best of his ability, always kept his word. He therefore trusted him and never blamed Jones when, finally, only a fraction of the money owed was forthcoming. Lunt noted that when Jones made application for wages and prize money, he placed against Henry Lunt's name the amount due the highest officers, exceeded only by the amount due the chevalier himself. Some money did come through, and now Lunt could go home with a measure of pride to a hero's welcome. When he left Philadelphia for his parents' home in Newbury, Massachusetts, where his wife and son awaited him, he had cash in his pouch. To be sure, it was only $387.40 of doubtful currency to show for three and one half years of recognized naval service. But what was money now to a hero whose sights were set on home.

It was a happy homecoming. They had prepared a fitting welcome for him. When word that the ship bearing him was anchored outside the bar at the Merrimack River's mouth, the townspeople gathered. There was no booming of cannon nor banging of church bells for security's sake, but they sent out a barge for him and a welcoming committee of local dignitaries.

By the time Lieutenant Henry Lunt, wearing his fine uniform with ruffles at throat and wrists, disembarked at the common wharf in Newburyport, the Market Square was well filled with people. Their huzzahs gladdened his heart and brought a flush to his weathered cheeks. To be so honored by his family, neighbors, and friends was best of all. Unaccustomed tears came to his eyes as he saw they had done it up right.

There were drummers and a fife or two from Joppy, fine carriages from the hill, and many a continental uniform from land and sea. Then the speeches began to welcome him officially home. They were of necessity short, it was said, but they took two hours. Forced to stand within sight of those he had longed to see for so long, and they in sight of him, emotions began to spill over. By the time his sobbing family was hustled toward him before the ogling townsmen, Lieutenant Lunt himself was openly in tears. He embraced his wife, Sarah, and their son, his father, Matthew, and his stepmother, Hannah. His eyes, darting eagerly about, found his brother, Captain Daniel Lunt, who stood with his cousin Richard who had preceded him home. Both stood grinning with hats doffed high in his honor. This broke the ice of restraint.

Dignity gave way to manifestations of joy, and he fell on the neck of his cousin, Cutting, whom he had not seen since the latter's recapture by the British from the jolly boat of the *Bon Homme Richard* off the coast of Ireland.

The role of hero came easily to the former lieutenant of the *Bon Homme Richard*, the *Serapis*, the *Alliance* and the *Ariel*, but it was short lived. After the celebration, there were questions to answer and interminable talk about events he would as soon forget. When he moved up close to his friends and neighbors, he became uneasy, and, finding himself out of step with their ideas of what had been and ought to be, he fell silent. This offended them, and they soon were telling one another that Henry Lunt had become strange, dandified, and somewhat conceited.

Lunt often wished himself capable of weaving for them a fabric of lies which would have pleased them better than the truth. He saw the quick exchange of glances and caught the innuendo. He told himself this was because more than half of the people he met he had never known before. Here were boys, as he had left them five years before, turned into men—their young faces strained into masks of bitter hatred by all they had endured through war's alarms.

Henry Lunt took particular note of those men missing from familiar places. Too many women, pale and unsmiling, wearing a mark of black on their garments, passed him deliberately on opposite sides of the street. It grew to be more than he could bear to inquire after either friend of foe; he dreaded so to hear the inevitable answer. Why, it seemed that half the town was either missing or known dead.

Lunt took some solace from the bosom of his family, but even his wife and sisters pressed him, and they prodded him to tell of the corrupt life at the naughty French court—if indeed he had been there. He was unable to oblige them, which caused them to doubt. Recalling bland-faced Louis XVI and his vivacious but regal queen, Marie Antoinette, he tried in a fumbling way just to please them, to describe an appearance at court. But, Henry Lunt was no John Paul Jones—descriptively articulate and poetic, able to paint vivid verbal pictures of the capricious life at the incredibly beautiful Versailles palace—even if he had been close enough to have firsthand knowledge.

There was a lighter, brighter side during this far too brief stay on land. It was nothing short of bliss to sit at the board and hear his father's voice beseeching divine blessing for the hearty, home baked meals prepared by the women. It was feast, indeed, to gaze upon his pretty, dark-haired wife who seemed to have aged not at all, and his blonde, rosy-cheeked son, now five years old, who would have naught to do with his stranger-father.

There were evenings all too brief when he sat with his brother Daniel (Ezra was still with General Washington's forces) and his male cousins before their various hearths while each told of his experiences. Since neither Cutting nor Richard could substantiate Henry's visit to the French court, there were many anecdotes and tales of John Paul Jones and the experiences they had shared.

They spoke in sadness of lives which had been sacrificed and of families left bereft and in want. With Captain Daniel Lunt entering in, they recalled the miseries of Old Mill Prison. Somehow, with melancholic reminiscences, the tone of their gatherings changed and became charged with ugliness. The vicissitudes of war had marked them more than they were capable of realizing. They were distressed but helpless before arguments which would arise in an atmosphere of almost total disagreement over who did right or wrong, more or less. Their meetings would end this way, and none could foresee the moment the mood of camaraderie changed to one of contention in time to prevent it.

In May, Henry Lunt received the letter that John Paul Jones had promised him in answer to his resignation submitted and declined at Corunna. When he read it, Henry was forced to smile, and he later had a hearty laugh with Richard, for Jones had not failed to mention Henry's belated boarding of the *Bon Homme Richard* during the *Serapis* fight. Henry declared, "It's a wonder he didn't include the one about Cutting and the jolly boat."

However, the letter was one to cherish. Henry carefully preserved it and proudly displayed it whenever asked. It, as well as his letter of resignation, is carefully preserved in National Archives of America.

Typical of Jones, the letter, clearly one of recommendation, was timed to serve as a reminder to Lunt that future service with Jones was in the offing. The letter read:

The bearer hereof, Mr. Henry Lunt, has served under my command on board the Continental ship *Bon Homme Richard*. He was first employed by me as a midshipman at L'Orient in the summer of 1779. He had been released from British prison by Cartel. I soon promoted him to the station of Second Lieutenant and he continued with me in that ship as such, and was with me in the ship *Alliance* from The Texel to France, and also thence with me in the ship *Ariel* to this Port as Second Lieutenant.

Mr. Lunt has been with me in many trying circumstances, and he has always behaved like a good officer, for which he has my best wishes.

He had not the good fortune to be on board at the time of the engagement with the *Serapis* till the close of the action. He is included with the vote of thanks which I have been honored with by the Congress since my return to this country.

                 Given my hand at Philadelphia, May, 1781
                 Chevalier Paul Jones

Before summer came fully on them, Henry Lunt took leave of his family once more. This time, he journeyed to Baltimore, where he saw to the outfitting of a ship of twenty-guns to be under his command, to bring to America goods from L'Orient.

In August of 1781, decisive actions of the American Revolution began to foreshadow victory for the insurrectionists. Probably unbelieving, and certainly unaware of the great strategy being planned against him, Lord Cornwallis concentrated his forces at Yorktown in Virginia.

That same month, unaware that he, too, was to be defeated by the war's end, John Paul Jones left Philadelphia by overland stage for Portsmouth, New Hampshire. Still officially on leave, he dallied on the way to pay several visits.

He visited General George Washington and the French General Rochambeau at White Plains, New York, where he dropped off dispatches of more personal importance than he dreamed. Ezra Lunt and his company were there, some of them in the famous Washington guard, but whether or not Jones looked him up is not certain.

Nevertheless, John Paul Jones stopped off at Newburyport on his way north to inquire after his old shipmates. He inquired after Henry and Cutting Lunt and was informed that he had missed seeing both men by only a few days. He expressed deep disappointment.

Henry had left for Baltimore, but Cutting was off on a cruise which would spell his end. The *Bon Homme Richard*'s fiery third lieutenant would never serve with John Paul Jones again, nor any other. He sailed on the privateer *America*, owned by Joseph Marquand and others, which with all hands, was lost at sea.

Jones visited the families of his former lieutenants and left messages asking both Henry and Cutting to contact him at Portsmouth whenever they should find it convenient.

Without further delay, the chevalier set out by stage for Portsmouth, arriving there in mid September. He was about to undertake one of the most challenging projects of his life, with defeat always lurking in the shadows about him and disappointment awaiting him at the finish. Jones supervised the fitting of the frigate *America* under very trying circumstances—under the very noses of the British, who now were maneuvering about off the New England coast.

Although somewhat belated in diligence, Britain had learned to take this obsession for a navy by her colonies very seriously, and she was three times as aggressive during the building of the *America* as she had been during the building of the earlier ships.

British naval ships made every effort to land raiders, whose purpose it was to destroy the *America*, but they were not successful. Many of their various plans were intercepted by spys lent to the Portsmouth area under the command of General Washington.

John Paul Jones organized an armed guard for the *America* and drilled some new recruits in the art of self-defense with the use of cannon. They had occasion to use both knowledge and equipment. When the British made several attempts to pass through the narrow gate of the Piscatauqua River to reach Langdon's Island and set fire to the *America*, they were foiled and fought off each time. Once again, the men were forced to conclude that a special Providence watched over the activities of John Paul Jones.

The chevalier was most happy to be reunited with his Portsmouth acquaintances, and he enjoyed the same rapport with them as he had done before when he had supervised the outfitting of the *Ranger*. In particular, it was a joy to discover his old friend, Major Hackett of Salisbury Point, Massachusetts, hard at work as master builder of the *America*. If Jones, now a recognized expert, saw flaws in the unchanging Hackett design and method, he was now the supremely polished diplomat with a penchant for achieving his ends without discord.

James Hackett, it is said, never saw a ship of the line. If so, it is all the more to his credit and to that of his brother, William, the designer, that their end products were the most beautiful and fastest warships ever. The long, low bowsprit of their ships was used for scores of years thereafter by the American navy.

The *America*, it will be remembered, was ordered in the Congress on November 9, 1776. The heaviest warship laid down in America during the revolutionary war period, she was the finest of her class and the first ship on the ways at Langdon's Island. So much controversy raged about her, so many were the suggestions as to her construction and outfitting, that the Marine Committee wisely shelved her actual building until after they had constructed the faster, lighter ships.

Everyone had a suggestion concerning the *America*. Even Captain Pierre Landais is said to have offered his opinions as to how she should be constructed, and some members of the earlier Marine Committee found his suggestions most acceptable. Had the *America* gone into the building stages early in 1779, the Landais plan might have been the one used. If so, she would have had two decks, with twenty-eight, twenty-four pounders in her lower battery and twenty-eight, eighteen pounders in her upper battery.

Major Hackett who, from the first, favored the smaller, lighter frigate, was not particularly intrigued by association with so large a sailing ship. In his thinking, he had the support of Josiah Bartlett and others. They protested that the Congress was putting all of its eggs in one basket. It would take nearly all of the men and supplies they had to stock the *America*, and there would be little or nothing left for the other ships.

While controversy raged, the *America* rested her ribs upon the ways. She was next heard of for positive action in 1781, when Robert Morris wrote that her speedy launching had been authorized and that the Congress had placed her under the command of John Paul Jones. When completed, she would be a seventy-four gun ship and another feather in the caps of James and William Hackett of Massachusetts and John Paul Jones of Virginia.

## 25

## THE *AMERICA*

The *America* was said, by some, to be the largest seventy-four gun warship in the world at the time of her building. At a distance of a mile, none could suspect that she had a second battery, so delicate was she in appearance.

The *America* was 182½ feet in length on her upper gun deck and 51½ feet in breadth. Her quarter deck projected four feet before the mainmast. Her forecastle was long and waist deep, with three gangways broad that were of equal height with the quarter deck and forecastle. There was just room for longboats between the gangways.

A breastwork pierced with gun ports, but of suitable height for musketry, was of the same strength and nature as the sides of the ship. It ran all around the quarter deck and forecastle and could be fought on the same side. This was an advantage held by no other ship of the times.

Above this breastwork, the poop deck stood on pillars eighteen feet long and projected eight feet before the mizzenmast.

Around the poop deck, a folding breastwork was made of light materials and of a strength to resist grape shot. When this breastwork was folded down on the deck, it could be raised in a minute so that it was impossible to perceive that the *America* had a poop at even a distance of a quarter mile.

With only single quarter galleries and no stern gallery, both her stern and bow were made very strong so that men at quarters everywhere were under good cover.

The figurehead of the *America* was both colorful and unusual. It was a beautiful female figure, head crowned with laurel, right arm raised with forefinger pointing to heaven. Its left arm presented a buckler with blue ground and thirteen stars representing the thirteen colonies. The legs and feet of the figurehead were covered, here and there, with wreaths of smoke to represent the dangers and difficulties of war.

There was other carved statuary. On the stern of the frigate, under the windows of the great cabin, loomed two large figures in bas-relief. One represented tyranny and the other oppression. They were unique in their presentation, being bound and biting the ground with the cap of liberty on a pole above their heads. On the back section of the starboard quarter gallery was a large figure of Neptune, and on the larboard gallery an equally large figure of Mars.

Over the windows of the great cabin on the highest section of stern was a large medallion containing a figure depicting wisdom surrounded by danger with the bird of Athens over her head. For emphasis, there appeared fearful darts of lightning.

The influence of John Paul Jones cannot be doubted, for it is next to impossible to believe that the creative influences adorning the *America* came from any other than his own poetic design. He labored and brought forth a ship equipped to forbid the presence of war and welcome the presence of peace. Such a magnificent vessel would bespeak a civilized and genteel America to the king of France, and he, Chevalier John Paul Jones, would be a fitting Mercury in the ancient language of all culture.

Such creativity was lost on the scrupulous provinciality of Major James Hackett, but he had learned to respect and admire the harder practicality of Jones, the shrewd and indomitable naval tactician. The two men, each so different from the other, worked harmoniously enough together, but certain other advisors resisted Jones and his ideas all the way.

There were innumerable delays in rigging and arming the *America*. It must be remembered that money was short, and workman had to be paid then, as now. Suitable workmen were not easy to come by in an era when master carpenters were carried aboard ship at excellent recompense, for there were not the repair shops nor repair ships available then. James Hackett never had more than twenty-four carpenters employed at one time, and he has been criticized for this by later day evaluators.

But, in all likelihood, he couldn't help it.

The *America* was nearly finished, and John Paul Jones now began to take steps to man her. At first, his quest was easy. The *America* was a legendary ship with all of the preposterous rumors surrounding her as to size and capability that the mind of man could devise. Jones dispatched a barrage of letters to his former lieutenants and lesser officers in which his descriptions of the *America* and her potentialities were vivid and glowing. He assured them that the great new frigate was the ultimate of all their dreams, and that each man would find his own ideas exemplified in the corrective details of construction.

The chevalier presented to his faithful followers a picture of an impregnable and indestructible ship. He had been confident all along that they would not refuse him. For once he was wrong, for refuse him they did. There is no evidence that there was any great rush of Jones's former seamates to Portsmouth. The reason for this was probably a combination of many things.

Henry Lunt was under negotiation with the Tracy family and laboring mightily to restore his lost resources. Cutting Lunt was on a voyage never to return. Richard Lunt was frankly disenchanted with American naval service. His view was shared by many others.

Many seamen who had served with Jones felt their previous expedition had failed, that they had done little more than tickle the toes of the British Isles and, the way they saw it, had done no more than lead the British fleet in a circuitous chase in the seas surrounding her coast. They had done this without profit. Whatever contribution they had made to independence and a war's end, they failed to see at this point in time. Richard Dale might have joined his former captain, but something intervened that spelled finish to Jones's dream of conquest and glory via the *America*.

An accident involving a squadron of French-line ships while approaching Boston Harbor was the deciding factor. This squadron was coming to America's aid. The celebration planned to welcome these ships-of-war was immediately dampened when one of their finest, the *Magnifique*, fouled on a shoal and was lost.

The Marine Committee met in panic and took hasty action endorsed by Congress. The king of France must be cajoled and recompensed so that word of such action would coincide with the advisement of his loss. It was voted to give the *America* to France. She would be called the *Magnifique*, named for the ship that had foundered. Robert Morris, a sponsor of John Paul Jones and Agent of Main, was assigned the painful task of breaking the news to Jones. He did so in a letter warmly and delicately worded.

Jones replied in restrained and typical gentlemanly fashion. His dignity moved Morris to reply:

Oct. 9, 1782

Chevalier Paul Jones, Portsmouth

Sir, I have received your letter of the 22nd of [September].

The sentiments contained in it will always reflect highest honor upon your character. They have made so strong an impression upon my mind that I immediately transmitted an extract of your letter to Congress. I doubt not but that they will review it in the manner which I have done.

And so ended a dream.

Paul Jones faithfully supervised the *America*'s building until she was launched in the cold of November 5, 1782.

It had been necessary to build this ship on the safest side of Langdon's Island not easily accessible to the British navy, and her launching would not be easy. Jones overrode all obstacles with his accustomed skill. The river was not more than 200 yards wide. On one side of the ship was a ledge of rocks running halfway across the river and parallel to the direction of the ship's keel. The opposite shore was fringed with rocks. The tide rushed rapidly in and out.

It was necessary to launch the *America-Magnifique* near flood tide, when the current was sweeping out swiftly and strongly to lend assistance in keeping the ship away from the rock ledge. Also, to obviate this, Jones had cables and anchors secured on shore, arranged so as to check the speed of the ship. It was an engineering feat of excellence and timing. Everything of a practical nature had been done to secure the safety of the magnificent frigate. The chevalier was ready.

Now, there must not be a launching without a fitting celebration. The word went out, and people gathered until there was a sizeable crowd. If there were those of the enemy about, they never made themselves known for fear of immediate and severe reprisal.

It was a proud moment. The flags of France and America were displayed together at the stern of the ship. Jones took his stand on a platform near the bow of the ship. He gave every signal, watched every move, and ordered when the anchors at the bow were to be let go in succession. Majestically and without a flaw, the great frigate slipped to the water. The watching crowd cheered long and lustily.

On that same day, Jones, with great dignity, surrendered the *America* to Chevalier de Marigne who commanded the *Magnifique*.

John Paul Jones couldn't bear to face his Portsmouth friends. Too proud to accept either their patronage or their condolences, he left town the day after the launching of the *America* on the early morning stage. He had boasted so freely of the future American navy and his role as leader, he was sick at the thought of his deprivation. He was far more disappointed than he cared to show.

Riding back over the narrow, bumpy stage route to Philadelphia, he paid no visits. Alone and unattended, he retired at various taverns along the way without fanfare and, for the most part, unrecognized. Actually, few in New England had ever seen him.

Perhaps he took refuge in dreaming, always his refuge and escape when harsh reality wounded his highly sensitive nature. Perhaps, as he rode in the huge stagecoach in rocking motion with eyes tightly shut, he imaged himself standing among his concealed cannon on the quarter deck of the *America*. Looking out into his yards, he saw that they were peopled with ruddy-faced Yankee seamen who met his stern appraisal with unflinching candor and a full measure of hero worship.

Oh, the beauty of that great and magnificent ship. Never was there such thunder from the heavens as emanated from those white, billowing sails as they caught and held the wind—wind so wild as to pound and punish and bear them along like an arrow shot through the wave until the helmsmen bent with aching arms and cried out for their relief.

Those two invincibles from Newbury, Massachusetts, Henry and Cutting Lunt, were up there in the tops with their boys, for never could they be persuaded to be elsewhere out of harm's way. The roars of Cutting could be heard above the din—the clank and the chomp as he vowed a speedy trip to Davy Jones to any who shirked. There was the performance of Henry, whose fearless antics on spar and line could set the chevalier himself on edge. Perhaps Jones could never have performed as well without them. Certainly, by his own admission, he missed them. In any case, the dream was not to be.

Jones had painted a glowing picture in many high places. He portrayed the *America*, his flagship, leading such a glorious American fleet (of American and French warships together) that the mighty fleet of Britain would be swept from her supremacy of the seas—a position she had held since Sir Francis Drake's defeat of the Spanish Armada in the time of Queen Elizabeth I.

During his rocky, overland journey from Portsmouth, Jones purged his thoughts and erased his dream for good. By the time he reached Philadelphia, he had recaptured a measure of his old optimism. He immediately sought out his friends, Robert Morris in particular, and received assurances from them that he would receive a new commission.

The chevalier was physically ill, a fact he was not yet ready to admit publicly. But he did contemplate retirement, and he decided to prepare for this in the early, if not immediate, future.

In December, 1782, there were well supported rumors that England was on the verge of surrendering totally in this war she had underestimated and was fighting on so many fronts. With France and Spain already lined up against her, she was really crushed, when, on April 17, 1782, Holland recognized the United States as a new and independent nation.

Paul Jones, with his usual shrewdness, saw the end in sight. He still wanted to be in on that end and to play a large role in the establishment of a superior American navy. He decided to put down some roots which he felt would make clear his position to those in authoritative positions. Expecting a large sum of money owed him from France (if he could believe his intelligence sources, and he always seemed to) he directed that an extensive estate be purchased for him in Newark, New Jersey. But he was not yet ready to retire.

The Honorable Robert Morris moved to give Jones command of a large and strongly built frigate called the *South Carolina*. This unusually fast and formidable ship had been protecting the coastline of South Carolina for about three years. Her commander, Commodore Gillon, had enjoyed his role as leader of a small flotilla and did not intend to give up his flagship. When he heard that the Congress had blithely voted to give the *South Carolina* to another commander, he balked. He would yield to Jones no more than to anyone else. Gillon put to sea.

The *South Carolina* had just about cleared the Capes of Delaware when she was pounced upon and captured by three English frigates, the *Diomede*, the *Astre* and the *Quebec*.

Then, Paul Jones was scourged by the irate South Carolinians for a lust after the best ships that had destroyed brave and successful defender of their coast in Captain Gillon. The red-faced supporters of Captain Jones retrenched and thought of a way to get themselves off the hook.

A French fleet of ten sail was then at Boston, there to be united with a combined French and Spanish fleet under Count d'Estaing. There were seventy vessels in this squadron. They were on the eve of departure to invade the island of Jamaica and take it from the British when Jones was given eleventh hour permission, at his own request, to join this force. Robert Morris influenced the Congress to pass a flattering recommendation for Jones, directed to the Marquis de Vaudreuil. The chevalier was received at Boston aboard the flagship of the Marquis, the *Triomphante*. It was a choice assignment and Jones did not hesitate simply because he was not to command the operation, to the relief of all concerned.

In spite of its pretentious beginning, the voyage was not a pleasant nor particularly successful one. Jones was among the many who took sick with an intermittent fever. Around the month of March, 1783, Jones wrote to a friend, John Ross, Esq., who was handling his business affairs for him and informed Ross that he would soon be returning. He asked Ross to negotiate for a permanent home for him.

The American Revolution was coming to a close. A cessation of hostilities was at hand that included participation by the nations of France, Spain, and Holland as well as America.

The definitive treaty was signed in Paris, France, on September 3, 1783. It stated:

1. The boundaries of America should be similar to those of the colonies under the Treaty of 1763 and the King's Proclamation of the same year; thus the northern boundary followed the southern boundary of Canada. From the point where the forty-fifth parallel reached the St. Lawrence River, it followed the channel of that river to the Great Lakes and connecting waters to the northwest corner of the Lake-of-Woods, and thence due west to the source of the Mississippi River.

2. That Congress would recommend the states to pass Relief Acts for the Loyalists.

3. That the United States was to have fishing rights off Newfoundland.

4. That private debts should be payable at the close of the war.

5. That the British armies were to be withdrawn at once from all posts in the United States, taking no Negroes with them.

6. That the navigation of the Mississippi River was to be free to subjects of both countries.

The expedition to Jamaica was the last action Paul Jones would participate in for America. He was on this for five months, after which he reappeared in Philadelphia on May 18, 1783, somewhat, but not so much, in the role of hero. But, the praise of his French companions was still ringing in his ears. He received commendations from both the Marquis de Vaudreuil and the Baron de Viomenil, communicated by them to France and to the Congress. They wrote of their admiration for the chevalier and stated that they were sentimentally touched by his obvious deep love of America and its flag.

Jones was in poor health indeed. He retired to Bethlehem, Pennsylvania, on the banks of the Lehigh River about sixty miles northwest of Philadelphia. Unfortunately for him, he remained there only a short time. Once his health started to improve (which it inevitably did during the few periods of time when he led a normal life), he was moved again into action by other motivation.

Paul Jones had not forgotten his loyal people of the L'Orient fleet, nor the fact that they still waited for the wages and prize money due them. He pressed his friends in the Congress to gain permission for his journey overseas to collect that money. On November 1, 1783, he was appointed Agent of the United States Government to collect prize money for prizes taken in Europe by ships under his command.

Moving fast, as was his custom, Jones sailed on November 10 from Philadelphia on the ship *Washington*. How quickly are old hates and old angers subsided. After a stormy passage of twenty days, he arrived at Plymouth, England in sight of Old Mill prison and was challenged by nobody. He proceeded to Paris, France, a journey of five days, where he was warmly welcomed. But he was dismayed at the condition he found there. Times were rapidly changing.

The beautiful Queen Marie Antoinette, never a favorite with the bourgeoisie, was now beset on every side by a bestial mood of intolerance. Aristocrats, not of her small, close circle, labeled her The Austrichen, the least of what she was being called in a lampooning by the scurrilous newspapers of the French underground. Mild, pedestrian Louis XVI was labeled a feebleminded, cuckolded pawn of his lascivious queen.

It was not easy within such an environment to ferret out who controlled the purse strings. It was discouraging to discover that the prize ships credited to Jones had all been sold and the money dumped into the fast dwindling French treasury.

The situation was an embarrassing one. Several years had passed. The sailors who had assisted in capturing those prize ships were either scattered throughout the world or dead. Without their presence on the spot, obtaining total prize money owed, or any part of it, was not going to be easy. However, after much dissembling and debate, when Jones was heartily sick and tired of it all, he was awarded a portion of the money due. It was all of it he would ever get, and he promptly sent the precise share of it to America for division among his people wherever they could be found. Paid on July 15, 1785, nearly two years after his arrival in France, Jones was awarded the sum of 181,039 livres, 1 sous, and

10 derniers. After that, the chevalier took a step which was to tarnish and diminish his image in America.

For reasons only guessed at—poverty for one—Jones allowed himself to be regarded as a soldier of fortune when he accepted the invitation of Empress Catherine of Russia to serve as an admiral in her Royal Navy. His service to Russia brought rewards from the empress, and it was hailed as equal to that of his service to America. However, it caused his name to become taboo—unmentionable—for more than two generations of Americans.

Many of those who served with him were more charitable, and Henry Lunt was one who chose to share in Jones's decline in popularity rather than apologize for his association with the chevalier.

John Paul Jones was too long forgotten, and historians missed the era when they might have salvaged an incredible biography of a great man. This remarkable sailor died at the age of forty-five and, within the framework of his short life, rendered his adopted country, America, his devoted service.

He was never vanquished at sea. He fought twenty-three sea battles. He made seven victorious ascents upon Great Britain and her colonies. He captured two warships of equal size and two of far superior size, with his own, besides taking many store ships and other craft. He forced the British to desist pillaging and burning in America, and to exchange, as prisoners of war, the Americans whom they had captured and plunged into prisons as traitors, pirates, and felons.

Thwarted throughout much of his life, called renegade and pirate, his sensitive spirit was dampened at the end when he heard his hard-won battles referred to as war crimes.

John Paul Jones died of a broken heart at a moment in time when the American navy he had fought to establish had all but disappeared. A century was to pass before the country he professed to love finally allowed him his place in history.

With the French Revolution, Paris, France, had become the scene of wild disorder. Small wonder that the death of John Paul Jones on July 18, 1792, received so little notice. The minister to France at that time, Gouverneur Morris, when notified that Jones had passed away, quickly advised the authorities to skip it.

He claimed that the times were not right for a public funeral for so controversial a figure.

There were a few others who could not accept this downgrading of a one-time hero. One of these was a Frenchman named Simmoneau, who happened to be the commissary to whom it was necessary to apply for a Protestant burial permit. Simmoneau expressed indignation at such neglect that Jones should be so abandoned even in death. It is claimed that M. Simmoneau opened both his heart and his purse, and that he, personally, paid for the funeral. At the same time, he predicted that America would one day have a change of heart and come looking for her great naval hero.

This is, of course, what happened—but it almost never did. For a long time, the grave of John Paul Jones remained truly lost. Then, 100 years later, during the administration of President William McKinley, the search for the long lost grave was undertaken. Full credit for this must go to the man who was McKinley's ambassador to France, Horace Porter. It was Porter who persisted, long after another less dedicated person might have given up. His task, therefore, was not an easy one.

Jones, having died in Paris where the religion was predominantly Roman Catholic, had not been buried in a large cemetery. He was buried instead in a small, Protestant cemetery named Saint Louis, in an area where angry, destructive revolutionists could work their ruin.

Porter's search began in June, 1899, but it was not until early February, 1905, that he was sure enough of his location to start digging. The operation attracted interest only because it offered competition to those citizens of Paris who made their livelihood engaging in the energetic occupation of dump picking. The Saint Louis cemetery had long since been lost under a city dump. Watching an engineering project that drove five or six shafts eighteen feet down into waste materials, the poor people subscribed to a rumor that a huge fortune was being excavated.

The grave of John Paul Jones was in a poor section of Paris, and his leaden coffin was discovered, finally, on March 31, 1905. The dump pickers lost interest at once when they discovered that the coffin actually contained a body rather than valuables. They went away scratching their heads over a government so rich that it could spend it's money to dig up one man.

The body of John Paul Jones was brought to America in all of the sterile pomp and circumstance of a Victorian memorial. This was brought about through the continued interest of Mr. McKinley's successor, President Theodore Roosevelt, a gentleman who believed in doing everything precisely and expeditiously.

John Paul Jones would have mightily approved the ceremony in his behalf. Finally, the two naval fleets, American and French, lay side by side as the chevalier had dreamed they would. However, not to engage in battle, but to honor the great and deserving naval hero himself. President Roosevelt had ordered a squadron of four battleships, under the command of Admiral Charles Dwight Sigsbee, "to proceed to Cherbourg and convey the body to America."

Home at last, rescued from a nameless grave, John Paul Jones now sleeps at Annapolis, an ever-present reminder of America's need for a "Respecktable Navy" to the young midshipmen who receive their training there. It is written upon his grave:

> He hath made the Flagg of America respected among the Flaggs of other Nations.*

---

* See Appendix F, on the death of John Paul Jones, eighty-five years after.

## 26

## THE TOLLS OF WAR

By the year 1781, the family of Matthew Lunt had fallen on hard times. The substantial accumulation of goods obtained through the efforts and hard work of five generations had been sacrificed in rebellion against a single tax.

It was the stamp tax, or was it the tax on tea? Matthew Lunt could not for the life of himself remember. All that he knew was that he was old and tired, and he was burdened with the families of Ezra and Henry Lunt. He had failed to acquaint Henry with his circumstances when this youngest son had returned home in August. He couldn't bring himself to do so and spoil the homecoming. Instead, he complained to his wife, who was stepmother to his children and had no compunction about berating the wives of both Henry and Ezra.

Ezra, being on land and nearer at hand, bore the brunt, and, in a letter, he assured his father that events of the near future would end his obligation. He did not say what the events were, but he either was privy to the American war plan or an excellent prophet.

In September of 1781, the French fleet under Count de Grasse entered the Chesapeake Bay. Washington, opposing General Clinton in New York, was aided by the French troops under Rochambeau. In a brilliant maneuver, General Washington took his army, in a series of rapid marches, into Virginia. At the same time, French and American columns under the command of Alexander Hamilton stormed other British defenses.

On October 17, 1781, when Washington confronted Lord Cornwallis at Yorktown, the British were being bedeviled by land and sea. Quite precipitately, with the enemy everywhere and all around him, the British general gave over his sword and is said to have surrendered seven thousand or more men—just about his entire army.

Soon after the victory at Yorktown, Ezra marched his company home to Newburyport, and he stopped on the way in Newbury at his father's house to scoop up his family. In a farm wagon with all of their goods, they were in the procession that entered the town to receive the traditional hero's welcome.

It was good to be home, and Ezra Lunt intended to stay. There was only one flaw. He was very short of money and owed considerable wages which were long in coming. In desperation, he pressured a loan and invested with a partner in a local tavern, where he was, for a time, successful.

His status as a revolutionary war hero remained untarnished until he again succumbed to war's blandishments and responded to another less popular call to help put down the Shays Rebellion. But that was later, and there was still more of the revolutionary war which demanded his loyalty and his service on the home front.

Henry Lunt was still running war supplies from L'Orient, France to America when there came another optimistic happening. On April 19, 1782, the sixth anniversary of the Battles of Lexington and Concord, Holland acknowledged the independence of the United States. John Adams had proved a most skillful diplomat and had done his work well. Now, he was hailed as the hero of the hour.

Influenced by the news of Holland's recognition and certain that the war was now over, Henry Lunt decided that he had done enough for his country and it was time he did likewise for his family. He returned to Baltimore on his last cruise, in July of 1782, and said a final good-bye to the Continental navy.

Lunt went home by overland stage, and the first person he met when he stepped down before the Wolfe Tavern was Captain Moses Davenport, a friend of his family. Davenport, a dedicated patriot still, did not trust Matthew Lunt to deliver a message which might once again drag Henry away. Over a table of hot toddy in the tap room, he informed Lunt that John Paul Jones, soon to command the fine frigate *America*, wanted a word with him.

If Henry Lunt crept surreptitiously away to join Jones at

Portsmouth, only to return when plans fell through, there is nothing of record to verify this. In fact, if the two ever met again, it was not as captain and master. However, it almost seems certain that Jones dispatched one of his famous letters to his former second lieutenant, having publicly declared his desire to have him as an officer on the *America*. Perhaps that letter was hidden or destroyed by Matthew Lunt—or possibly Sarah Lunt. It is even possible that Henry Lunt said his farewells to Jones at Portsmouth after the *America* was given to France. Due to Captain Davenport's intervention, there is a scant bit of evidence that that was what really happened. In any case, the fate which conspired to bring together two men who looked alike, from opposite sides of the sea, to fight in a common cause, now conspired to separate them forever.

Despondency of spirit, and fear of the future were the two enemies Henry Lunt could not overcome. As the years moved along, he went less and less to sea, turning to familiar scenes and familiar faces in the hope that they would ease his mind.

Sitting at table in Ezra's tavern, with a mug of rum always his companion, Henry listened to the complaints of his contemporaries, and he brooded. It didn't help that his attire was now as threadbare as those about him while he lived with the agony of men nursing war wounds which would never heal. He heard men express discouragement and anger at the scarcity of living materials as well as bitter condemnation of a government so impoverished it hadn't even paid off its army.

The government hadn't paid off its navy either, but Henry Lunt withdrew to a lonely taking of the opposite view, clinging yet to a thread of hope that John Paul Jones would come through for him. He asked of Ezra, "Are all men mercenaries, now?"

Ezra was swift to reproach his brother, reminding him that an able sea captain could still earn rich rewards, while those in supportive land operations could not.

Henry became sullen at the arguments Ezra would use. He had seen no rich rewards, with merchants taking more and more and captains less and less. A captain now must own at least a part of his ship to make trade worth his while. Goaded by Ezra's constant nagging, Henry frequently stayed too long at the tavern, and the longer he stayed the more argumentative he became. The liquor seemed to muddle his brain, and he developed the irritating practice of speaking derisively in a jargon of English and French combined. He was gaining a reputation for being more than slightly mad.

Many a night, under cover of darkness, Captain Daniel Lunt lurched up from the Water Street tavern with Henry, a burden of drunkenness, on his arm. Had Daniel lived, there might have been a leveling off of tempers by daylight, but he did not. In that same year of 1787, he succumbed to the lingering illnesses brought on by hardship and imprisonment. Sadly, they laid him to rest in the Newbury churchyard.

In spite of his problems, Ezra Lunt did his best to constructively serve his country during the painful years of the reconstruction. When serious rebellions within the impoverished communities threatened anarchy, he rallied once more to the call to arms. In the year 1786, he led a company out of Newburyport to help put down the Shays Rebellion at Worcester, Massachusetts.

The rebellion was not without cause, but its purposes were impractical. It sought to overthrow the courts of the land that were prosecuting delinquent debtors (many of them war veterans) and to force the issuance of paper money without regard for its redeemable potential.

Fortunately, the rebellion was of comparatively short duration, and, in something under six months, on July 2, Ezra Lunt returned home. He had not been away for long, but long enough to place himself in serious financial jeopardy. He then went all out to collect at least a part of his war wages which were still outstanding. In this activity, he was prodded constantly by his subordinates who felt that he should speak for them also.

The town fathers were in a hassle of their own and not inclined to listen as they once might have. For fifteen years the selectmen of Newburyport had been trying to gain recompense out of the federal government for monies they had spent in defense of the coast during the war. In particular, did they attempt to recover from the Commonwealth of Massachusetts for the fort built on Plum Island and the piers sunk in the Merrimack River. To lend substance to all their claims, they repeatedly pointed out that the Newburyport Harbor had been a refuge, and for a considerable time the only safe nothern point where American ships and their prizes could come in.

Requests for reimbursement began in the year 1776 and continued persistently through 1790. The last such futile request was made of the Commonwealth in the spring of 1789. That petition, dated May 16 and signed by the selectmen of Newburyport, was recognized in the House of Representatives on June 20. There, the matter ended. No money was ever paid.

Ezra Lunt realized that what the town fathers could not do, neither could he. He was tired of fighting other men's battles. He was tired of contending and being at odds with his brother, Henry. He began to listen to those who were urging him to pull up stakes and travel west.

Distinguished contemporaries in the American Revolution, General Rufus Putnam, Samuel Parsons, and the Reverend Manasseh Cutler, were among those spearheading plans to bring organization and government to the Northwest Territory. They formed a company and invited Ezra Lunt to come along. Their aims were very acceptable. They promised:

1. Civil rights and religious liberty with representative government.
2. Admission to the Union as soon as inhabitants numbered sixty-thousand free persons (not less than three and not more than four states to be created out of the total territory).
3. No slavery or involuntary servitude other than the punishment of crime.
4. The thirty-sixth section of each township was to be put aside to aid education.
5. There would be division of estates among all heirs.

Within this territory, Ohio had been settled in 1788, and, in 1790, Ezra Lunt decided to go there. He was never sorry.

Ohio was a state of dense forests and beautiful waters, quickly capturing his stalwart heart. He felt he could breathe freely once more, and his only regret was that so little of his life stretched ahead of him. Ezra Lunt lived happily in Ohio for twelve years before he passed away in 1803. That same year, Ohio was admitted to the Union.

Henry Lunt did not like the turn of events in France, and when the French Revolution was set in motion on July 14, 1789, with the storming of the Bastille in Paris, he saw all of his war service as an exercise in futility.

His moods of deep despondency increased when his brother Ezra moved away to Ohio, and he lived in constant fear of the overthrow of the new American government. As his years at sea came to a close, he found that he had little money and few resources. With an increased family of five children to support, he pushed his years of sea duty beyond what his worn-out body could stand.

All hopes for receiving the wages and prize money due him ended when he received word of the death of John Paul Jones in Paris. The money Jones had sent from France for distribution among his men had long since disappeared into the American government coffers.

Ailing in body and mind, Henry Lunt allowed himself to become mired in the role of pariah, until even the boys in the street hooted and laughed behind his back. As he stayed at home more and more, his maladjustment to his native town of Newburyport became more and more evident. He felt the eyes of his neighbors upon him from behind lifted curtains as he passed their houses. He met their derisive sneers when face to face in public places.

Henry Lunt offended his fraternal brothers of long standing in the oldest lodge of Masons in Newburyport when he appeared at meeting "washed as was his won't, but drunk," and stood up to declare that the first presiding officer of the lodge had been a mercenary engaging in privateering for personal gain during the late war.

He offended his fellow members of the Newburyport Marine Society at every hand to such an extent that they collected the fire buckets donated by him and his family for the protection of the town and returned them to him.

When level-headed sea captains of his own generation pressed him for more stable behavior, he told them he was a citizen of France and further fanned their resentments by offering to install a guillotine with which they could chop off his head.

Possibly he was on the verge of madness, as some declared,

but it is certain that he was tormented and bedeviled on all sides. In the heat of a new time and a new attitude, Henry Lunt saw around him sea captains of a new generation. In the agony of old age, he saw that they were of the same young age that he had been at Philadelphia that long ago, cold January of 1776, when, fired with vigor and optimism, he had elected to serve aboard the flagship *Alfred* under the young Lieutenant John Paul Jones.

To this young group, Henry Lunt was simply old. If he spoke softly of his own experiences in an effort to help them, they scoffed at old solutions to new problems. If he raised his voice to be heard, protesting the continuance of war and killing, they whispered that he was a coward and a pacifist. By the time he realized that they did not wish to hear him, he was bruised in spirit beyond recovery.

Receiving no comfort from his contemporaries, for there were few left who had paralleled his experiences, he began to stay away from meetings of the Newburyport Marine Society. When they sent a delegation to his home to remind him that his dues were unpaid, he had his wife tell them he was sick in bed. Henry Lunt was expelled from the Newburyport Marine Society for "having absented himself from this Society, paid no attention to summons, failure to pay dues and other notorious behavior."\*

As the years of his life grew short, Captain Henry Lunt suffered great disillusionment and bitterness of spirit, although he was, to a degree, sustained by the memories of the exhilarating life at sea when he was always a winner. Nothing, neither ridicule nor privation, could erase the memory of the glorious triumphs of his passionate involvement with the sea and the country he loved. He, likewise, deeply loved and was thankful for his devoted wife, Sarah. The tragedy of their marriage was that five years was probably all they actually had together.

After her husband's death in 1805, at the age of fifty-two, Sarah Lunt had a most difficult time making ends meet, and she survived him by thirty-three years. She was a genteel lady, but one whose pride yielded willingly to the needs of her children. She picked up the fight for wages and prize money due her

---

\* See Bibliography, item 11.

husband. It was never forthcoming. Sarah Lunt did receive a tiny pension, but not until this was awarded to every widow of the revolutionary war. In the meantime, she never gave up in her efforts to obtain what was due her husband.

Incredible as it may seem, there was an unwillingness in high places to accept the right of Henry Lunt's claim, for it was in the years when the country wanted no reminder of men who had served with John Paul Jones. Proper authorities refused to even glance at the letter of recommendation written by Jones for Henry Lunt. Sarah was then required to gather affidavits from prominent citizens of Newburyport who remembered the young and estimable captain.

Captain Moses Davenport* was most assuredly one of Newburyport's most illustrious natives, and he was most generous in his affidavit for Mrs. Lunt, made before a justice of the peace in Newburyport, declaring that:

> ... said Paul Jones called upon me. Jones had come to Newburyport to make inquiry after said Lunt. On being informed that he was absent, Captain Jones expressed extreme regret.
>
> He stated he was then on his way to Portsmouth, N. H., on business for the government.
>
> He said his objective at that time in making inquiry for Captain Lunt was to determine whether the government might not reavail themselves of his service.
>
> Jones spoke of Lunt's service on the *Bon Homme Richard* and remarked that he should prefer him as an officer in the service to any he had known.

Other affidavits were provided Sarah Lunt, but none were more telling than that of Captain Davenport. These were admitted by the government as argument for a just claim. It must have been a humiliating experience for the gently reared lady and her children.

Eventually the United States government endorsed her claim,

---

\* See Bibliography, item 12.

and the widow's pension was allowed. Up to the time of her death, Sarah Lunt had received $1,435.60 or $41.02 for each year after her husband died.

The United States of America was fifty years old, and the Black Hawk Indians were making war against whites out in Illinois when Sarah (Orcutt) Lunt died in the year 1833. She had lived through four major wars and the election of six presidents. The thirteen original colonies had been augmented to twenty-four.

The endless procession of major and minor conflicts that ensued in the name of freedom had no power to excite her. For her, no other war ever existed such as that of the American Revolution which had robbed her of a husband and father. Expecting separations as the wife of a seafarer, she had not counted on the long separations of war and imprisonment or their wretched aftermath.

She had begun her married life at the first a lonely wife and then a lonely mother. Even so, she was a dutiful helpmate according to the prescribed attitudes of the times in which she lived. She existed in her marriage through an exchange, with her husband, of long and affectionate letters. It was a safe, sweet and impregnable dream world; in the end, one more endurable than the shorter, tangible relationship that came too late. She might have denied it, but Sarah Lunt was spiritually rejuvenated when Henry Lunt died. She accomplished this rejuvenation by receding into the past. There she dwelled complacently to a ripe old age while her contemporaries departed this life one by one.

She outlived all of those who would pity or patronize her, until, at the last, she had her hero as her young heart had seized and held him. The image of Henry Lunt, captain of the sea, second lieutenant of the *Bon Homme Richard*, emerged again for his devoted Sarah—strong, handsome, young, and untarnished.

# *Appendix*

## Appendix A

## Nathaniel Tracy

The Newburyport man who probably invested the most in privateering during the revolutionary times was Nathaniel Tracy, son of Patrick Tracy, a wealthy merchant and ship owner.*

In 1775, a time of general upheaval, before the congressional action, Nathaniel Tracy is credited with having "fitted out the first privateer ever sent out by his country."

Other statistics revealed by several historians are astounding if true. Twenty-three of Tracy's fleet of privateers bore letters of marque and carried altogether 298 guns and 1,618 men.

He sent out 24 cruising vessels and 2,800 men.

His grand total was 47 vessels, 638 guns, and 4,418 men.

His ships brought home 120 enemy vessels, and 2,225 prisoners with prize money amounting to $3,900,000 in gold.

Nevertheless, he lost both money and ships by the war's end, and he died a comparatively poor man.

Newburyport, it is said, within seven years, lost one quarter of its whole population in privateers who sailed away, never to return. Apparently, a few eventually returned after confinement in British prisons.

---

* The red brick home built by Patrick Tracy for his son, Nathaniel, is now the Newburyport Public Library.

## Appendix B

## Letters Documenting Jones's Trip to Newburyport

Two letters document Captain John Paul Jones's trip to Newburyport in 1776. Both were written by Commodore Hopkins; the first to Jones, the second to John Bradford.

Providence, R. I.<br>18 June 1776

To Captain Jones
Commander of the Providence
at Newport, R. I.

Sir: I have received orders that you proceed to Boston in the room, Newburyport. You are to make all dispatch there you can. The ships of war are driven out of that Bay, and I believe that Port is safest to send in Prizes, if any, on the Continent.

I am your Friend,<br>Esek Hopkins, Commander in Chief*

Providence, R. I.<br>28 June 1776

To John Bradford

I received your letter of the 17th instant. I had before given orders to Captain Jones of the Providence to sail for Newburyport. I shall send an express immediately to Newport, if she is not sailed, to proceed directly to Boston. There

---

* *American Archives*, 4th Series, Vol. VI, p. 972.

being no coal in this government, I think it will be best to bring what you can with you. Please send a line to Captain Jones at Newburyport to come to Boston, or where you think best, if he has sailed before my express arrives at Newburyport. . . .

>I am with great respect,
>your humble servant
>Esek Hopkins*

This visit by Jones to Newburyport ties in with Henry Lunt's visit home in June, 1776. It was not the first visit by Jones to that town.

On May 18, 1776, he was ordered to convoy a vessel with a cargo of cannon from Newburyport to New York City at the request of General George Washington.

There is evidence that Jones, on that occasion, picked up the convoy outside Newburyport Harbor, not wishing to foul on the piers sunk in the mouth of the Merrimack River.

---

* *Ibid.*

## Appendix C*

## The Privateer *Dalton*

### Officers**

Captain ................ Eleazer Johnson
First Lt. ................ Anthony Knapp
Second Lt. ............... John Buntin
Master ................ Daniel Lunt

Complement
120 Men

*Newburyport*
Capt. Eleazer Johnson, escaped
1st Lt. Anthony Knapp, escaped
2nd Lt. John Buntin, escaped
Daniel Lunt, Master, escaped
Alexander Ross, escaped
Offin Boardman, escaped
Moses Cross
Thomas Cluston, escaped
Cutting Lunt, *Bon Homme Richard*
William Bradbury
Henry Lunt, *Bon Homme*
Joseph Racklief
William Shackford, *Alliance*
John Key, escaped
John Barringer, escaped
———Stickney
Joseph Poor, *Alliance*
Nathaniel Warner
Josiah George
Moses Merrill
Jacob True, *Bon Home Richard*
John George
Richard Lunt, *Alliance*

* See Bibliography, items 2 and 3.
** All from Newburyport.

*Richard*
Samuel Cutler, escaped
Francis Little
Joseph Asulier, escaped
Joseph Brewster, *Bon Homme Richard*
Nathaniel Wyer, escaped
John Knowlton (cashier) died or escaped
Charles Herbert, *Alliance*
Joseph Choate, *Alliance*
Edward Spooner, joined British man-of-war-
Benjamin Carr, *Alliance*
Samuel Woodbridge
Ebenezer Hunt, dead

*Portsmouth, N. H.*
Nathaniel Marshall
Benjamin C. Stubbs
Jacob Nutter
George Triffering
Benjamin Babb, escaped
John Abbott, joined British man-of-war
Joseph Shilaby, *Alliance*
Guppy Studley

*Kittery*
John Foster, dead
Hugh Kenniston, escaped
Peter Tobey
John Perkins, *Bon Homme Richard*
Richard Seward
Nathaniel Seward
Stephen Lawley
Samuel Fletcher, *Bon Homme*

Ebenezer Brown, *Alliance*
Paul Noyes, *Alliance*
Joseph Plummer, *Alliance*
Reuben Tucker
John Smith, *Alliance*
Henry Smith
Ebenezer Edwards, *Alliance*
Jonathon Whitmore, joined British man-of-war
Thomas Bailey, *Bon Homme Richard*
Nathaniel Bailey, *Bon Homme Richard*
Daniel Cottle, dead

*Berwick*
Tobias Weymouth
Gideon Warren, dead
Thomas Hammett, *Bon Homme Richard*
Thomas Rines, dead
Ebenezer Libby
Ichabod Lord, *Bon Homme Richard*
Aaron Goodwin
John Higgins
Andrew Whittam, *Alliance*

Samuel Stacey, *Bon Homme Richard*
Joshua Casell, *Bon Homme Richard* killed *Serapis* Battle
William Lewis, *Bon Homme Richard*
Nathaniel Kennard, *Bon Homme Richard*
Thomas Mahoney, *Bon*

*Richard*
Jacob Brewer
Nathaniel Staples
Ephraim Clark, *Alliance*
Samuel Scriggins, dead

*New Gloucester*
Asa Witham, dead
Zebulon Davis
Daniel Lane, escaped
Benjamin Yolin, *Alliance*

*Cape Porpoise*
John Burbank, *Bon Homme Richard*
Israel Lasedel

*Windham*
John Simpson, *Alliance*
Andrew Templeton

*Boston*
Joseph Clark, British man-of-war
John Bass, British man-of-war
Robert Burgoyne, escaped
Joseph Hatch, dead

*Hampton, N. H.*
Dr. Samuel Smith, escaped
Elisha Johnston
Ichabod Shaw

*Homme Richard*
Winthrop Willey
Daniel Knight, *Alliance*
George Fernel
John Gunnison, *Bon Homme Richard*

*Old York*
James Sellers
Tobias Sellers
Timothy Harris
John Downs, *Bon Homme Richard*

*Block Point*
William Maxwell
Samuel Carroll, *Alliance*
John Maddon, *Bon Homme Richard*
Joseph Burnham
Samuel Smith

*Cape Pursue*
Nathaniel Porter
Jacob Wyman

*Casco Bay*
John McCoffey
Isaac Leajor

*Salem*
James Lawrence

*Virginia*
William Ford, British man-of-war

*Scotland*
Adam Ladley

*Marblehead*
Bonner Darling, dead

*England*
Clement Woodhouse

*Ireland*
Henry Barrett, escaped
William Smith, British man-of-war
William Horner, British man-of-war

## Appendix D

## The Treaty of Alliance with France, 1778

This treaty was the work of Benjamin Franklin. It provided for:
1. French acknowledgment of American independence
2. Offensive and defensive alliance against England
3. Guarantees of possessions of both in America

Without France, the Americans could never have won their independence. Without the alliance, England could have better dealt with other European powers. As it was, she ultimately became involved in a general European war.

Without Benjamin Franklin, it is most apparent there would have been no alliance with France. Builders of the American nation were keenly aware of this.

Franklin was appointed "Minister Plenipotentiary" to France, America's first foreign minister.

## Appendix E

## The American Squadron

| Ships | Complements | Captains |
|---|---|---|
| Frigate *Bon Homme Richard**  | 380 | John Paul Jones, USN** |
| Frigate *Alliance* | 215 | Pierre Landais, USN |
| Frigate *La Pallas* | 253 | Nicoles Cottineau |
| Corvette *La Vengeance* | 66 | Lt. de Philippe Nicholas Ricot |
| Cutter *Le Cerf* | 157 | Ens. de V. Joseph Varage |
| Privateer *Monsieur* | 357 | Guidloup |
| Privateer *Granville* | 100 | Dumaurier |

* Flagship
** Commodore

## Appendix F

### On the Death of John Paul Jones Eighty-five Years After
(as recorded in the *Newburyport Herald* on March 1, 1877)

It was eighty-five years ago last Wednesday that John Paul Jones of Revolutionary memory died. If the Turks had one man like him, it would more than double the efficiency of their whole Navy.

He fought the enemy on the ocean and pushed into the harbors of England and Scotland to cut out their ships and bombard their towns; but his greatest exploit was the capture of the *Serapis* with the *Bon Homme Richard*.

In the fight were four\* Lunts from Newburyport, and we understand that the Lunt family intend this year to celebrate the anniversary of that battle.

---

\* There may have been four members of the Lunt family with John Paul Jones. I have found only three. I could find no record of a celebration by that family in March of 1877.

## Appendix G

## Old South Church

The Old South Church of Newburyport, Massachusetts, stands much as it did in Ezra Lunt's day.

White paneled box pews, a gallery on three sides, footstools, and arm boards mark it's age.

The high pulpit is the one from which the famous eighteenth-century evangelist, George Whitefield, preached, and his bones are interred directly under it.

Facing the congregation on the wall on either side of the pulpit are two giant marble slabs. One proclaims in large letters the story of the forming of Ezra Lunt's Company and is inscribed as follows: "In its broad aisle April 25, 1775 Major Ezra Lunt enrolled the first company of volunteers enlisted for the Revolutionary Army."

## Appendix H

## Tristram Dalton

Tristram Dalton was the son of Michael and Mary (Little) Dalton and was born in Newburyport on May 28, 1738.

A graduate of Harvard College in 1755, he married on October 25, 1758, Ruth, daughter of Robert Hooper of Marblehead.

Prior to the Revolutionary War, when he became active as a patriot, he engaged successfully in agriculture and commercial endeavors.

On the organization of a federal government in 1789, after the adoption of the Constitution of the United States, he was one of the first two senators to represent Massachusetts. He was wealthy at that time. Dalton, still wealthy when he took his seat, was poverty-stricken at the time of his death in 1817. His more than comfortable home is now the quarters of a select club which bears his name on State Street, Newburyport.

Records of visits to the Dalton House by Washington, Lafayette, and others are carefully preserved by its members, who enjoy displaying its relics to a stream of tourists each year.

## Appendix I

## Dr. Ezra Green
### Ship's Surgeon of the *Ranger*

Dr. Green, born in Malden, Massachusetts, on June 17, 1746, graduated from Harvard College and studied medicine under a Dr. Sprague of Malden and finished his course under a Dr. Fisher of Newburyport. He went to live in Dover, New Hampshire, in 1767.

His wife, the former Susannah Hayes of Dover, whom he married December 13, 1778, following his return to Portsmouth in October aboard the *Ranger*, found her young years full of an absentee husband, who, on March 12, 1779, was still writing her how much he missed her, even though duty still called him. Dr. Green was but one of thousands of patriots who placed their country first. His first service was in June, 1775, when, on the Sunday following word of the Battle of Bunker Hill, he became one of the first American Army surgeons.

# BIBLIOGRAPHY

1. *Lunt Family of America*, a genealogy compiled by Thomas S. Lunt.
2. Journal of Samuel Cutler, clerk of the privateer *Dalton*, July 12, 1777, includes the complement of the *Dalton*. Ref: *New England Genealogical Register*, vol. 32, pp. 42, 48, 184, 305; vol. 28, p. 187; and vol. 19.
3. *Charles Herbert Diary*. He served on both the *Dalton* and the *Alliance* and provided further documentation of the complement of the *Dalton*, a list of men and their ships from Old Mill Prison and sketchy lists of names of other Americans on the *Alliance* and *Bon Homme Richard*. The *Charles Herbert Diary* in its original state was once at the Cushing House, Historical Society of Old Newbury, but now only a copy is there. It was published in 1854 by Pierce of Boston under the title, *The Prisoners of 1776; A Relic of the Revolution* by Rev. R. Livesey.
4. *A History of the United States Navy from 1775 to 1893* by Edgar Stanton Maclay, A.M., vol. 1, p. 109. Concerning Americans coming from British prisons for exchange and not British prisoners, as some historians have claimed.
5. *The American Archives*. "A collection of authentic records, state papers, debates, letters and other notices of publick affairs." It was prepared by Peter Force and published under the authority of an Act of Congress. It was begun in 1837 and halted when the appropriation of money ran out. Most of the letters and documents concerning John Paul Jones's correspondence with Joseph Hewes, Robert Morris, Benjamin Franklin, and others are contained in these huge volumes of fine print. Both Henry Lunt's letter of recognition from Jones and his letter of resignation are contained therein. Included also is the ordeal of Capt. Daniel Lunt when captured by the British, Fourth Series, vol. 5, p. 759.

Ref: Vols. 2 and 3, Fifth Series; vols. 1 through 6, Fourth Series.
Letters of the Rhode Island Navy, particularly those of Commodore Esek Hopkins, are found in vol. 2 of the Fifth Series.

6. *Emmon's Statistical History of the U.S. Navy of Official Documents.*

7. Map of Newburyport Harbor, surveyed in 1826 by Lt. Col. J. Anderson, army engineer, used for descriptions of the harbor. It was then very wide and deep, with the channel sweeping out in the direction of the south breaker where the Catholic Church now stands on Plum Island.

8. Newburyport Town Records, vol. 1, pp. 237, 239, 241, tells of batteries on Plum Island and wooden piers sunk in the river Merrimack near Black Rocks in 1775.

9. *Ships of the Past* by Charles D. Davis. James Hackett of Amesbury, Massachusetts, was ordered to Portsmouth [New Hampshire, then Massachusetts] by the Continental Congress to build ships for the United States government.

10. *The Court Martial of Peter Landais.* Ref: Mss Division, Library of Congress, Washington, D.C. The Papers of the Continental Congress, vol. 11, p. 193.

11. Henry Lunt was expelled from the Newburyport Marine Society in 1799, "having absented himself from this society, paid no attention to summons, failure to pay dues, and otherwise notorious behavior." Ref: History of the Marine Society of Newburyport, published 1906, p. 312.

12. Captain Moses Davenport, co-owner of the Wolfe Tavern, Newburyport inn and favorite meeting place [see Chapter 1]. He was a son of William Davenport, who converted his dwelling into the inn, frequently known as Davenport's Inn. Ref: *A History of Newburyport, Mass.* by John J. Currier, vol. 1, p. 387.

13. *Diary of Dr. Ezra Green,** surgeon of the Continental ship-of-war *Ranger.* Ref: Public Library, Dover, New Hampshire.

14. Letter of William Whipple to Josiah Bartlett, [signer of the Declaration of Independence from Amesbury, Massachusetts, a section now Newton, New Hampshire]. Ref. *New England Genealogical Register*, vol. 30. Revolutionary War Letters begin on p. 303.

* See Appendix I.

*Other References:*
   *War of the Revolution* by Jacob Abbott.
   *The Life and Correspondence of Miss Janette Taylor,* 1747-1792.
   *Reminiscences of Elisha Atkins* by William H. Reed, pp. 18, 97.
   *Memorials of the Society of Cincinnati of Massachusetts* by Francis S. Drake. Excerpt: "Capt. D. Lunt is enlisted as a member of the Society and the First Regiment of Massachusetts."
   *Diary of a Yankee Privateersman.* Excerpt: "Monday, September 5, 1778. This day, we have it in the newspaper of Boston of the *Providence* and *Ranger* having taken fourteen merchantmen with the convoy, a frigate, and have sent them into France. [This was during Jones's famous cruise of the Irish Channel.] Ref: Massachusetts Archives, vol. CXC111.

*Other Sources*
   Public Libraries of Newburyport, Ipswich and Boston, Massachusetts, Portsmouth, Dover and Concord, New Hampshire, and the Essex Institute, Salem, Massachusetts, and Russell L. Jackson, director emeritus.